Highlights

The ULTIMATE ON-the-GO Activity BOOK

KID TESTED BY
→ Remy Garofano (age 7)
→ Lillian McMullan (age 11)
→ Isla McCloud (age 11)

HIGHLIGHTS PRESS
Honesdale, Pennsylvania

Packing List

- [ ] Toothbrush, paste, & floss
- [ ] Clothes, socks, & underpants
- [ ] Shoes
- [ ] Snacks
- [ ] Reusable water bottle
- [ ] Sunscreen
- [ ] Earbuds
- [ ] Pen & plain paper
- [ ] Deck of cards
- [ ] Piggy bank stash
- [ ] Hairbrush
- [ ] Markers
- [ ] Comfy PJs
- [ ] Sunglasses
- [ ] Neck pillow

4

1
ALL
ABOUT
YOU

30

3
TRAVEL
ADVENTURES

On-the-Go Survival Tips

FEELING CARSICK?

Take calm, deep breaths and focus on your breathing. Look out the window and set your gaze on one thing in the distance. Try cracking the window for fresh air, sipping water, or resting your head on a pillow. If none of that works, see if the driver can stop so you can walk around a little.

GOING TO A PLACE WHERE YOU DON'T KNOW THE LANGUAGE?

Before you leave, learn some greetings and common phrases in the local language. Practice saying these on your way to your destination. Once there, don't worry about getting something wrong. People are usually just happy to hear you trying to speak in their language.

FORGOT TO PACK SOMETHING?

If it's something small, maybe you can buy a replacement on the way. If not, see if you can make a substitute—for example, your sweatshirt could double as a neck pillow.

EXPERIENCING JET LAG?

Get lots of rest before your trip. Once you arrive, try to get on the sleep schedule of the local time zone as soon as possible. Dehydration can make jet lag worse, so drink plenty of water.

SITTING FOR TOO LONG?

During car trips, make sure to stretch your arms and legs at pit stops. If you're on a plane or a train, get up every couple of hours and walk down the aisle.

CONTENTS

Take This Book with You!

Your bags are packed, your ride is here—it's time for a trip! And whether you're going by car, plane, train, or something else, this book is the perfect travel companion.

Arriving at your destination isn't the only fun part of traveling. Getting there can be an epic adventure, too. This book will help turn your trip into a super fun, action-packed, laugh-out-loud journey. It will provide ways for you to take in cool sights, let loose with your travel buddies, and keep busy during long waits.

Inside, you'll find puzzles, quizzes, multiplayer games, writing and drawing activities, and much more. The book is divided into eight chapters, but you don't have to go through them in order. Skip around, work backward—it's up to you how to use this book! Ready for the adventure to begin? On your mark, get set, go!

ALL ABOUT YOU

A Quiz About You

Circle T for every statement that is true and F for every one that is false.

T F ① It's impossible to sneeze with your eyes open.

T F ② Your earlobes are made mostly of fat.

T F ③ Sweat is made up of water, salt, and a splash of lemon juice.

T F ④ It's impossible to tickle yourself.

T F ⑤ People with curly hair smile more.

T F ⑥ A person can survive about 20 days without eating but only a few days without drinking.

T F ⑦ People's eyes stay the same size throughout life, but ears and noses don't stop growing.

T F ⑧ When your stomach is gurgling, it means it's high tide in your intestines.

T F ⑨ More than half the bones in the human body are in the hands and feet.

T F ⑩ The pinkie, or little finger, has the strongest muscle in the human body.

THIS ᴏʀ THAT

Circle the word in each question that best describes you.

Sweet or Salty?

Drawing or Painting?

Movies or TV Shows?

Sports or Music?   Messy or Clean?

Dogs or Cats?   Dancing or Singing?

Pancakes or Waffles?   Pop or Rap?

Summer or Winter?

5

I Think I'll Try...

Take this quiz to find out which hobby you might enjoy. Start at the top and work your way down.

I prefer to make

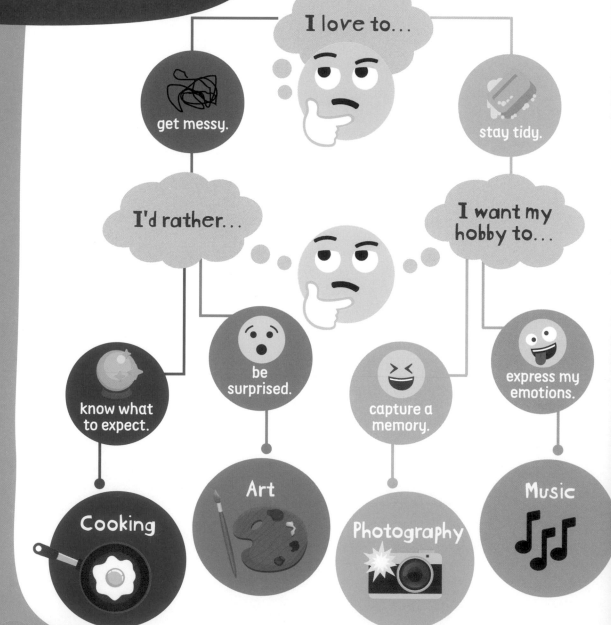

heart

I love to...

get messy.

stay tidy.

I'd rather...

I want my hobby to...

know what to expect.

be surprised.

capture a memory.

express my emotions.

Cooking

Art

Photography

Music

6

decisions with my...

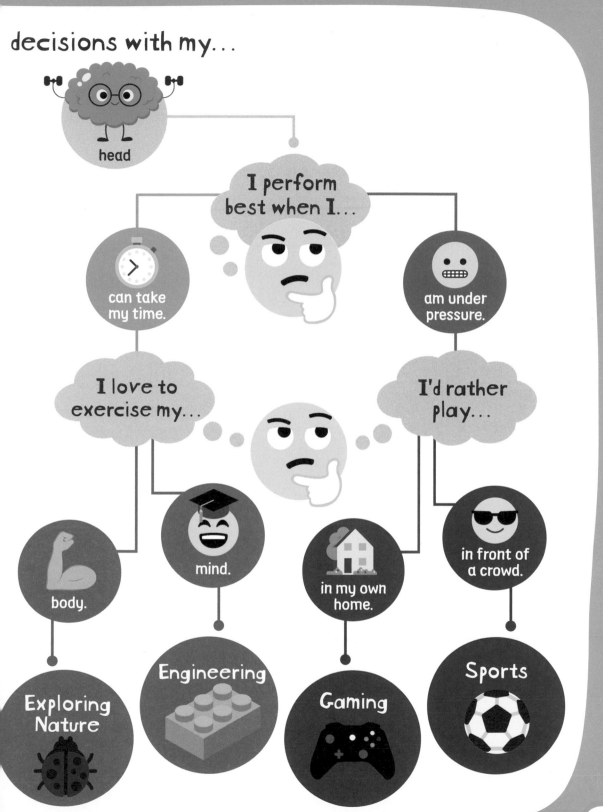

head

I perform best when I...

can take my time.

am under pressure.

I love to exercise my...

I'd rather play...

body.

mind.

in my own home.

in front of a crowd.

Exploring Nature

Engineering

Gaming

Sports

Family Flag

Design a family flag. What should be on it? Think of things that represent your family—it could be something you all enjoy doing, a favorite family meal, or anything you share together. Use symbols, colors, shapes, or whatever you want in your design. Then write your family motto. A motto is a short saying that expresses a person's or group's likes or values. For instance, you could go with "Always Be Kind!" or "Pancakes for Life!"

"PANCAKES FOR LIFE!"

"RIDE THE WAVE."

"ALWAYS BE KIND!"

FAMILY MOTTO:

Have you ever wanted to be a superhero? Step into a superhero's shoes by choosing your superhero name, extraordinary power, and outfit.

Send in the Superhero

Superhero Name

CHOOSE YOUR BIRTHDAY MONTH

JANUARY: The Great
FEBRUARY: Captain
MARCH: The Amazing
APRIL: Doctor
MAY: The Fantastic
JUNE: Professor
JULY: The Flying
AUGUST: Commander
SEPTEMBER: The Unstoppable
OCTOBER: Agent
NOVEMBER: The Invisible
DECEMBER: The Mysterious

THEN CHOOSE THE FIRST LETTER OF YOUR FIRST NAME

A: Guinea Pig
B: Green Bean
C: Cheese Stick
D: Marshmallow
E: Hullabaloo
F: Sandwich
G: Spinach
H: Jelly Bean
I: Sock
J: Broccoli
K: Kerfuffle
L: Puppy
M: Walrus

N: Cactus
O: Armadillo
P: Malarkey
Q: Pinecone
R: Platypus
S: Kitten
T: Waffle
U: Shenanigan
V: Scrambled Egg
W: Sloth
X: Gecko
Y: Guacamole
Z: Flapjack

Pick Your Power

Which animal do you relate to most? Pick one, and then see which superpower you should have.

CHEETAH = SUPERSPEED
DOLPHIN = AMAZING SWIMMING ABILITIES
FALCON = ABILITY TO FLY
GECKO = INCREDIBLE CLIMBING SKILLS
OCTOPUS = ELASTIC BODY
OWL = SUPERHEARING

Dress to Impress

Draw your superhero outfit here.

Fill in the Blanks

Three words that help describe me:

_____

_____

_____

Something I recently tried for the first time and liked:

_____

Something I'm good at:

_____

_____

Something I used to like, but not anymore:

_____

Two times when I felt very happy:

_____

_____

_____

My favorite indoor activity:

_____

_____

My favorite outdoor activity:

_____

_____

My favorite spot to be alone:

_____

My favorite food:

_____

My favorite smell:

_____

My favorite music right now:

_____

_____

_____

A sound I can imitate:

_____

A place I'd like to visit:

_____

If I could be an animal for a day, I would be:

_____

The kindest person I know is: _____

My most unusual talent:

_____

_____

_____

11

Draw Yourself

Look at your reflection in a window or take a selfie and draw a self-portrait using either as a guide.

Now draw what you think you'll look like 20 years from now!

13

TRAVEL GAMES

Games to Pass the Time

These games can be played out loud during any type of travel—in a car, bus, train, plane, or even on a rocket ship if you ever find yourself aboard one!

What if . . . ?

What if cars had swimming pools in the back? What if dogs could fly airplanes? What if people had four arms? Pose these questions to your travel companions and brainstorm the possibilities. Then take turns creating your own "what if" questions.

Questions, Questions

In this game, everyone speaks in questions. One person asks a question. The next person answers the first question with another question. The third person answers the second question with a different question, and so on. Let's say someone asks, "Who is the president?" The next player might respond, "Haven't you seen the news?" See how many questions your group can string in a row. You can make the game more difficult by adding a time limit or eliminating players who make a statement instead of asking a question.

Guesstimation

This is a game that you can change to suit where you are and what you feel like guessing on. For instance, if you're in a car, you and the other passengers might guess on how many out-of-state license plates you'll see in the next five minutes. Or if you're about to drive over a bridge, you can guess on how many red cars will pass you coming from the opposite direction. If you're on a train or in a plane, you could guess on how many people wearing blue shirts will pass your seats within a certain amount of time, and so on!

Games

Fortunately, Unfortunately

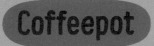

As you probably know, the word *fortunately* means "luckily," and the word *unfortunately* means "unluckily." This game creates a group story whereby each player adds both fortunate and unfortunate events. The first player begins a sentence by saying *fortunately*, followed by a description of a happy event. The same player quickly says *unfortunately*, followed by a related but unfortunate happening. Each player builds on the last player's contribution. Try to make it as silly as you can. For example:

PLAYER 1: Fortunately, I rode my bike to Canada. Unfortunately, I got a flat tire.
PLAYER 2: Fortunately, I had a spare tire tube. Unfortunately, space creatures stole my tire pump.

A, My Name is Anna

The first player has to say a sentence with an *A* name, an *A* place, and an *A* object. For example: "My name is Anna and I came from Alabama with a load of avocados." The second person must do the same thing but with *B* words. For example:
"My name is Brandon and I came from Boston with a load of boogie boards." Continue like this all the way through the alphabet.

Alphabet Search

In this multiplayer game, everyone looks around for a word that starts with the letter *A*. The word can appear on a road sign, on an airplane napkin, or wherever. When someone sees an *A* word, they say it aloud. Then everyone looks for a *B* word, and so on, going through the rest of the alphabet.

Coffeepot

This guessing game uses verbs as mystery words. One player silently chooses an action verb, such as *run*, *dance*, or *fly*. The other players ask questions to find out what the verb is—but when they ask questions, they replace the mystery verb with the word *coffeepot*. For example, they could ask, "Can you *coffeepot* at the table?" or "Can birds *coffeepot*?" Players may ask as many yes or no questions as they want to figure out the word.

My Ship Goes Sailing

One player begins by thinking of a favorite thing, such as horses. The player says, "My ship goes sailing with horses." The next player chooses another thing, such as jump ropes, and says, "My ship goes sailing with horses and jump ropes." The third player says the same sentence and adds another item. Players keep adding new items until one person forgets to say one of the items or gets them in the wrong order. That person is out. The last remaining player is the winner.

My Cousin Owns a Store

A player starts by thinking of an item—any noun. They say, "My cousin owns a store, and they sell something that begins with a *C*," or whatever letter is at the beginning of the player's item. Everyone tries to guess what it is. "Cantaloupe?" "Canary?" "Clarinet?" When someone guesses correctly, it's that person's turn to say, "My cousin owns a store, and they sell . . ."

Categories

One player chooses a category, such as dinosaurs, countries, or candy. Each player names something that belongs in that category. So, for dinosaurs, players could say *Triceratops*, *Stegosaurus*, *Tyrannosaurus rex*, and so on. Players continue like this until no one can think of any more items for the category or until someone repeats an item already named. Then begin the game again with a new category.

Tiger in Your Tank

The first person starts with the letter *A*. They say, "I have an apple in my attic," or any sentence that has an object beginning with *A* and a place beginning with *A*. The second person uses *B*. So, they could say, "I have a blueberry in my balloon." Keep in mind that your sentences *don't* have to make sense!

Games

3 Signs, 3 Minutes

This game works best in a car. Ask someone (but not the driver) to time you for three minutes. In that time, you and your opponent look for signs with numbers on them, such as speed limit, exit, and route signs. When you spot a sign, say the number out loud. If you are the first to say it, you get to write it down. Add it to the next numbered sign that you claim, and then the next one. Whoever gets the highest total from three different signs in three minutes is the winner.

City, State, Country

The first player chooses a city, state, or country and says it out loud. The next player must think of a city, state, or country that begins with the final letter of the first name. For example, if the first player says, "Boston," the next player could say, "Nebraska." Then the player after that could say, "Alabama" or "Australia." Players continue taking turns. If a player can't think of a place with the correct first letter, they're out. The last remaining player is the winner.

Virtual Hide-and-Seek

One person thinks of a place in the world to "hide" and doesn't tell any other players. The rest of the travelers in your group try to figure out where they are "hiding" by asking yes-or-no questions. You can decide the maximum number of questions that players can ask before the hider reveals where they are.

Stoplight Baseball

This game works best in a car. To play, passengers take turns being "at bat." The person at bat scores a run whenever the car you're in passes under a green light. Stopped at a red light? That's an out. Stop signs count as outs, too. After three outs, it's the next player's turn. The player with the most runs after an equal number of turns wins.

I Spy

The first player starts by saying, "I spy with my little eye something . . . red" (or any other color they see). It could be a red car, red leaves, or someone wearing a red shirt. The other players call out red things they see until one player gets it right. Then it's that player's turn to spy something.

Guessing Game

This game is a way to keep a young sister or brother happy. To play, ask your young sibling questions that you know they'll know the answers to, such as, "Who in the family has a birthday in June?" or "Which room in our house has a bunk bed?" Ask questions about your family, your home, your siblings' friends, or whatever you want. It can keep a younger child engaged and make them feel good.

Zip

Before the game starts, a player chooses a number between one and nine, and tells everyone what it is. To play, take turns counting. The first player says "one," the next says "two," and so on. When you come to any number that contains the chosen number, you must say "zip" instead of the number.

For example, if the chosen number were three, you'd say "zip" instead of 3, 13, 23, and any of the 30s. If you get caught not saying "zip" when you should, you're out. If you want an extra challenge, say "zip" if the number is a multiple of the chosen number (3, 6, 9, 12, etc.). Or say "zip" if the digits add up to the chosen number (12, 21, 30, 102, etc.).

Traffic Check

Look closely at the vehicles on this highway. The traffic on the left side of the highway is almost exactly the same as the traffic on the right. But there are a few differences.

For example, the blue-and-white tractor trailer on the left is longer than the blue-and-white tractor trailer on the right.

Can you find 11 other differences between the two sides of the highway?

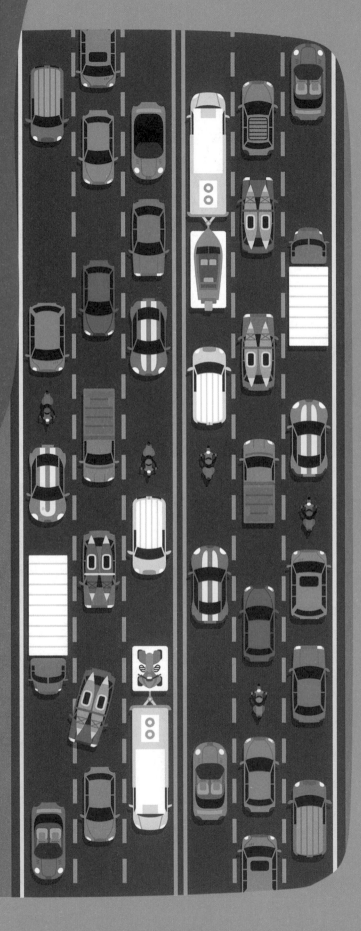

Car Trip Bingo

Car Trip Bingo is a two-player game. Each player chooses one grid for a bingo board. Whenever a player spots an item shown on the board, they use a pencil to place a small check next to it. The winner is the first player to spot five items in a row on their grid, either across, down, or diagonally.

taxi	bumper sticker	stop sign	tunnel	moon
cow	diner	pay toll sign	police car	motorcycle
traffic light	dog	FREE SPACE	mountains	barn
gas station	hotel	bridge	drive-thru restaurant	red car
speed limit sign	yard sale sign	body of water	moving truck	horse

	red car		pay toll sign	
body of water		school bus		bridge
gas station	hotel	drive-thru restaurant		dog
			taxi	
yard sale sign	cow	FREE SPACE	traffic light	speed limit sign
police car	stop sign	camper van	bumper sticker	moon
horse	mountains	barn	motorcycle	diner

Stay on Track

Can you find at least one thing that starts with each letter of the alphabet in the scene below? Hurry, before these critters have to run off to catch their trains!

TO TRAINS

TO TRAINS

TICKETS

TO TRA

TICKETS

FIRE

All Together Now

In these activities, you'll work as a team to create awesome art and stories.

Double Doodle

You and a travel buddy each doodle something quickly, then switch papers and add to each other's doodle. Keep switching and adding until you've turned the doodles into something or until you've filled up the pages.

Creature Feature

Fold a blank piece of paper into four sections, back and forth. The first player draws the head of a creature on the top section, and then folds it under so other players can't see the drawing. The next player draws on the second section, and then folds that back before handing it to the next player. Continue until all sections are used. Then unfold the paper and see what you've created!

Silly Stories

This game is for at least three players. The first player writes the first sentence of a story on a blank piece of paper and folds the paper just below the sentence. The second person reads the first sentence, writes the next, and folds the paper again. The third person can only read the sentence written just before their turn. Continue playing, with each person only looking at the line before the one they're writing. Together, decide when to write the last line, then unfold the paper and read your story!

And to this day, I have not eaten brussels sprouts!

Bear Hotel

The vacationers at the Great Grizzly Lodge are feeling bear-y cozy! Can you find the 12 hidden objects in the scene below?

SPECIAL HIBERNATION RATES

sock

toaster

hammer

harmonica

toothbrush

open book

banana

magnet

canoe

ladder

mushroom

anchor

Laugh Attack

A wonderfully weird board game!

Read the directions below. Then turn the page, lay the book flat, and begin the game.

For four to six players.

TO PLAY:

1 Tear out a game piece for each player and 7 triangles (2 yellow, 2 blue, 2 green, and 1 red) from page 143. Place the game pieces on START. Put the triangles in a hat, empty bag, or other container. Also grab a pen or pencil and some scrap paper.

2 When it's your turn, close your eyes and pick a triangle from the container. Then move your piece to the next unplayed space of that color. If you get to a space that's:

BLUE OR YELLOW: Complete the writing or drawing challenge that's given, using your scrap paper. Earn 2 points.

RED: Do the action written on the space. Lose a point (if you have any).

GREEN: Act out the scenario to earn a bonus point.

3 The first player to reach FINISH earns five points. Once all players reach FINISH, the player with the most points wins.

TURN PAGE TO PLAY

DRAW ME

Laugh Attack

ACT OUT
The call of a newly discovered bird species called the Tiny-Winged Honker

DRAW
The world's weirdest plant

WRITE
The name of a rather unappetizing new restaurant

WRITE
A name for your nose, elbow, or big toe

OH NO!
You've forgotten your own name. Let the player to your right give you a nickname.

ACT OUT
A terrible smell entering your nose

ACT OUT
A seagull eating some french fries dropped in the sand

DRAW
A robot with an incredible hairstyle

WRITE
A caption for this cartoon

OH NO!
You've been turned into a frog. Let out a loud *ribbit*.

OH NO!
You sneezed during your school photo. Make a sneezing face.

I THINK I'LL NAME MY NOSE SNIFFANY.

ALL ABOUT ONIONS!

OPEN

AAO

START HERE.

START

RIBBIT!

28

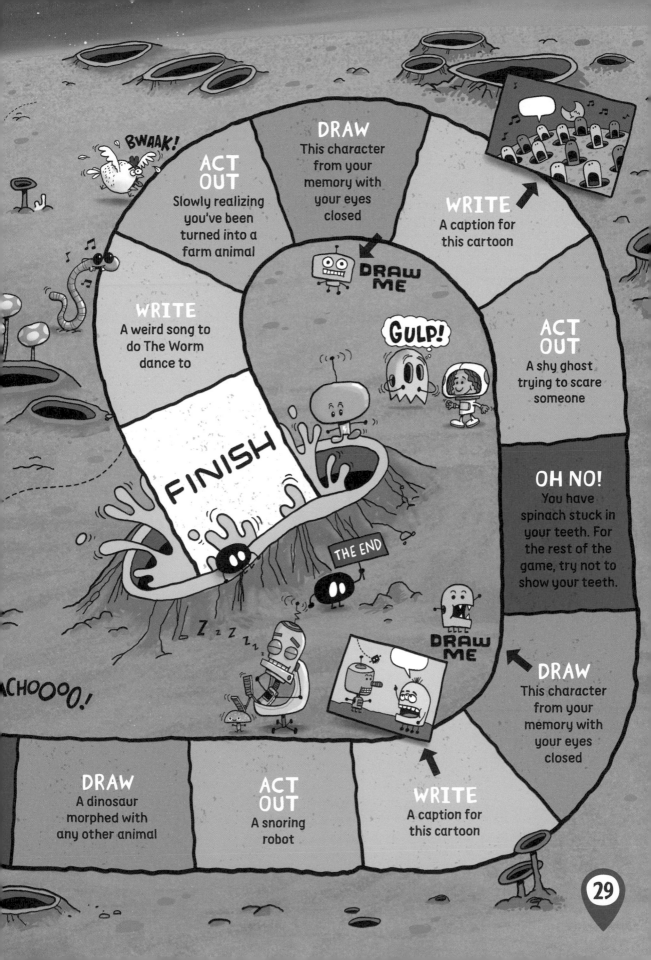

TRAVEL ADVENTURES

My Family

_____
NOUN

This is best played with a travel buddy. Without letting this person read the story, ask for the words or phrases under the blanks. For example, the first thing you'll ask for is a "friend's first name." After you've filled in all the blanks, read the story out loud.

Dear _____,
    FRIEND'S FIRST NAME

We just had the best family vacation! Everyone came along except _____,
        SIBLING'S/COUSIN'S NAME

who we had to put in a kennel. First, we _____ all the way to the
        VERB (PAST TENSE)

Museum of the American _____. It was _____! Did
        BODY PART   ADJECTIVE

you know that humans used to have three _____? Then we went to
        SAME BODY PART (PLURAL)

_____ World. We had to wait _____ hours in line to
  FRIEND'S LAST NAME   HIGH NUMBER

get on the "Rocket to _____ City" ride, but it was so worth it! I hurt my
        APPLIANCE

left _____ on the way down the last drop, but I was okay after Mom
    NOUN

rubbed _____ on it. Then I got the chance to _____ a
    FOOD YOU DON'T LIKE   VERB

giant _____! That was awesome, but its breath smelled like deep-fried,
    TYPE OF INSECT

_____-year-old _____. And that was just Monday!
  HIGH NUMBER   NOUN (PLURAL)

I'll write again soon to tell you about the rest of the trip. Bye!

What's Wrong?

Time for an undersea adventure. What wacky things do you see? It's up to you!

32

Rock It

These rock climbers got their ropes tangled. Can you set them straight? Follow each rope from the climber on the mountain to find out who their partner is.

On-the-Go Magic Show

Turn your trip into a magical extravaganza with these super fun tricks.

Math Magician

1. Ask a travel buddy to pick any number without telling you what it is (example: 13).

2. Have them add 5 to it ($13 + 5 = 18$).

3. Tell them to multiply that new number by 3 ($18 \times 3 = 54$).

4. Have them subtract 9 ($54 - 9 = 45$).

5. Tell them to divide that number by 3 ($45 \div 3 = 15$).

6. Have them subtract the original number from the new number ($15 - 13 = 2$).

7. Tell them you'll now "magically" guess the result, and say it's 2. (The trick is that the answer is always 2 with this math activity!)

"Remove" a Finger

1. Bend your left middle finger and right thumb like this.

2. Place your bent thumb on top of your bent middle finger.

3. Curl your right index and middle fingers around to cover the gap between your two bent fingers.

4. With your left palm facing you, pull your right hand away from your left to "remove" the top of your middle finger. *Eww!*

Now You See It, Now You Don't

The first four steps show how the trick looks to you.

1 Hold a quarter in front of you with your right fingertips. Say, "Observe that I have a quarter in in my hand."

2 Put your other hand in front of both the quarter and your fingertips so the audience can't see them. Say, "Before your eyes, I will make it disappear!"

3 Open the fingers of your right hand slightly, and let the quarter drop into your palm as you look at your audience and say, "With these magic words . . ."

4 Pretend that you are grabbing the quarter with your left hand as you say, ". . . and these magic powers . . ."

The last two steps show how the trick looks to the audience.

5 Hold your left fist out to the side while pointing toward it with your right hand. Say, ". . . the quarter will disappear."

6 Keep pointing with your right hand as you wiggle your left hand and say whatever magic words you want to use. Then say, "One, two, THREE!" Open your left hand wide to reveal that the quarter is gone!

PRACTICE THESE TRICKS AS MUCH AS YOU NEED TO BEFORE PERFORMING THEM!

Where in the World?

Hop around the globe with these guessing games!

First Flight

Joey, Haley, Talia, and Colin live in Oregon. This summer, they will each fly on an airplane for the first time. Use the clues to figure out where each one is going.

CLUES

- Joey is flying out of the United States but will not cross an ocean.
- Haley will fly east across an ocean.
- Talia will travel farther east than Haley.
- Colin will travel farther than Joey but will not fly out of the United States.

Vancouver, Canada

Paris, France

Hometown: Portland, Oregon

Orlando, Florida

New Delhi, India

What Am I?

This is the second largest one on Earth. It has the world's longest river. Its highest mountain is Kilimanjaro. To find out what it is, write the correct letters in the blank spaces, and then read down.

My first letter is in **PAT** but not **PET**. _____

My second letter is in **SAFE** but not **SANE**. _____

My third letter is in **CARE** but not **CAME**. _____

My fourth letter is in **LIT** but not **LET**. _____

My fifth letter is in **LACE** but not **LAME**. _____

My sixth letter is in **BAT** but not **BET**. _____

What am I? _____.

State Scramble

The names of six U.S. states are scrambled below.
Can you unscramble the letters?

WELCOME TO OH AID

1. WE MIX ONCE = _____
2. ANIME = _____
3. DOOR COLA = _____
4. HONK RAT TOAD = _____
5. IT'S NO NAME = _____
6. OLDER DANISH = _____

Postcard Riddles

Match each postcard message to the landmark it's describing.

1. Hi! This place is all it's cracked up to be. Sending hugs!

2. Ooh la la! I fell in love with this place. It's magnifique. Thinking of you!

3. I want to sing with joy! This place strikes the right note. Toodles!

4. She's so big up close. Are you green with envy? Wish you were here!

5. This place is fit for a king! Mummy and I are happy to be here. Miss you!

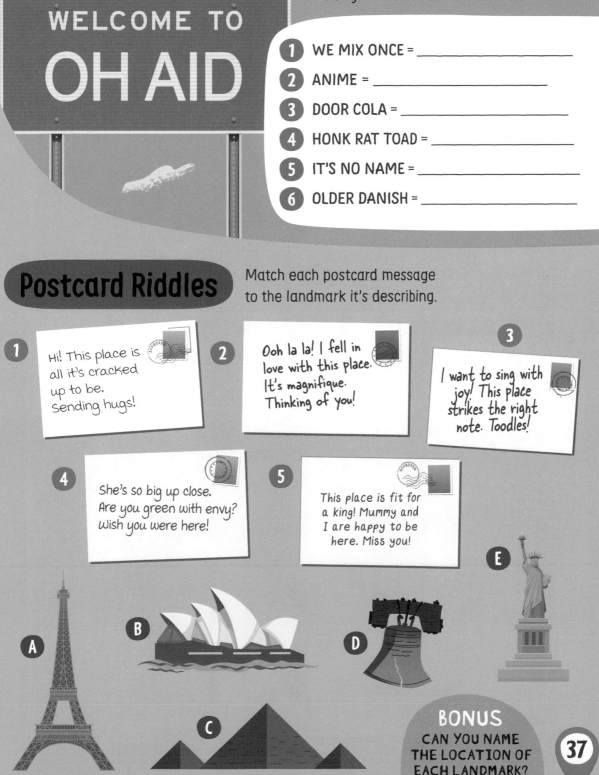

A
B
C
D
E

BONUS
CAN YOU NAME THE LOCATION OF EACH LANDMARK?

Balloon Bonanza

Up, up, and away!
Find at least 12 differences
between these two pictures.

Brave the Cave

These spelunkers are making some incredible finds. Can you find the 21 objects hidden in the scene below?

sock

carrot

bowling pin

button

tack

comb

snake

envelope

teacup

adhesive bandage

ice-cream cone

crescent moon

pencil

artist's brush

ice-cream bar

ruler

glove

slice of pizza

potato

yo-yo

frying pan

Park Here

The United States has dozens of national parks. The names of 33 of them are hidden in this grid. Can you find them all? They are hidden up, down, forward, backward, and diagonally. (The state abbreviations are not included.)

WORD LIST

ACADIA (ME)
ARCHES (UT)
BADLANDS (SD)
BIG BEND (TX)
BISCAYNE (FL)
CONGAREE (SC)
CRATER LAKE (OR)
DENALI (AK)
DRY TORTUGAS (FL)
EVERGLADES (FL)
GLACIER BAY (AK)
GRAND CANYON (AZ)
GRAND TETON (WY)
GREAT BASIN (NV)
HALEAKALA (HI)
HOT SPRINGS (AR)

ISLE ROYALE (MI)
JOSHUA TREE (CA)
KATMAI (AK)
MAMMOTH CAVE (KY)
MESA VERDE (CO)
MOUNT RAINIER (WA)
OLYMPIC (WA)
REDWOOD (CA)
ROCKY MOUNTAIN (CO)
SAGUARO (AZ)
SEQUOIA (CA)
SHENANDOAH (VA)
WIND CAVE (SD)
YELLOWSTONE (ID, MT, WY)
YOSEMITE (CA)
ZION (UT)

GREAT SMOKY MOUNTAINS (NC, TN)

```
S Z N G R A N D C A N Y O N E S M
N I P M O U N T R A I N I E R N A
O O R O R T E L A Y O R E L S I M
Y N D R Y T O R T U G A S Y N A M
R O S A L A K A E L A H G E G T O
O W S E D A L G R E V E A L R N T
C C I E D E N A L I E G J L E U H
K K O N M A T R A P N R O O A O C
Y E R N D I S D K B Y I C W T M A
M R S T G C T E E I A X I S B Y V
O J K L Z A A E F G C Y P T A K E
U I O V O I R V S B S R M O S O B
N A J S D U R E E E I S Y N I M A
T M E A H E Q J E N B G L E N S D
A T C G D U C D G D B J O Q Z T L
I A N W O R A S A G U A R O B A A
N K O I A N O T E T D N A R G E N
X O A B V V Y A B R E I C A L G R D
D Y H A O D N A N E H S S I V G S
M E S A V E R D E S E H C R A O B
```

National Park Adventures

- See the flashy colors of Grand Prismatic Spring at Yellowstone National Park.
- Scuba dive along the kelp forests of Channel Islands National Park.
- Scale one of the more than 8,000 climbing routes at Joshua Tree National Park.
- Spy on colorful gila monsters, a type of lizard, at Saguaro National Park.
- Camp under the northern lights at Denali National Park.

41

Happy Hiking!

As Mike hiked with his family, he wrote about their day. Later, he noticed that each sentence contained an item they took on the hike! Can you find a hiking item hidden in each of the sentences below? Hint: All the items are in the scene.

EXAMPLE: Like all good hikers, we left the trai**l unch**anged. (lunch)

1. Emma planned the route.

2. We stopped to sketch at the bridge.

3. Two squirrels came racing along a log!

4. The whole crew ate raisins for energy.

5. We came upon chopped trees near a beaver dam.

6. Our entire crew went slow at challenging, rocky parts of the trail.

BONUS! How many squirrels can you find in the scene?

Compass Code

To answer the riddle, start at the North (N) circle. Then move in the directions listed and write the letters you find in the correct spaces.

Compass grid letters:
```
    Y  T  A  E  B
    R  D  N  I  C
 W  X  O  H  W  F  E
    M  O  T  A  S
    K  R  U  D  E
```

1. S 1 _____
2. SE 2 _____
3. W 3 _____
4. NW 1 _____
5. S 3 _____
6. NE 3 _____
7. W 1 _____
8. S 2 _____
9. N 1 _____
10. SE 2 _____
11. W 3 _____
12. N 1 _____
13. E 2 _____
14. NW 2 _____

WHERE'S THE BEST PLACE TO EAT WHILE HIKING?

Where there's ____   ____ ____ ____

____ ____   ____ ____ ____ ____ .

Tic Tac Castle

What do the castles in each row (horizontally, vertically, and diagonally) have in common?

Cool Castles to Visit

PRAGUE CASTLE
CZECHIA

MATSUMOTO CASTLE
JAPAN

NEUSCHWANSTEIN
CASTLE
GERMANY

Hidden Words

Surf's up! There are six words (not pictures!) hidden in the scene below. Can you find SPLASH, SURF, SWIM, TOWEL, WAVE, and WET?

Speaking of Surfing...

Say each tongue twister three times, fast.

WILLY'S WET SUIT WHIPS OVER THE WAVE.

SAM WILL SWIM AFTER STEPH AND SETH SURF.

TERRY TOOK PERRY'S TEAL TERRY CLOTH TOWEL.

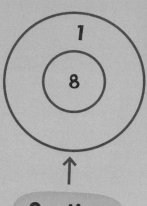

Curling

Place a dime in the space below to use as your curling "stone." Give it a gentle push with your finger.

SCORING: 1 point if the dime touches the outer circle; 8 points if it touches the inner circle.

Backseat Championships

Compete in these sports competitions—all from the comfort of your cushy seat! Grab a pencil and dime and follow the instructions for each game. Play on your own or with a travel buddy. Then add up your points and check the score box to see which medals you've won.

← Start

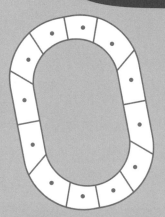

Slalom

Set a timer for 10 seconds. Using your nondominant hand, draw a line that curves around each of the dots (like the dotted line shown).

SCORING: 1 point for every dot your line curves around without missing.

Speed Skating

Close your eyes. Make one pencil dot in each of the 12 sections of the track (as shown).

SCORING: 1 point for each section that has one (and only one) pencil dot in it.

↑ Finish

↑ Start

↓ Start

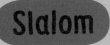

0 / 4 / 5 / 10 / 0

Ski Jump

Place your pencil on the ramp near Start. Close your eyes and draw a line, stopping when you think you've reached 10. SCORING: Get the number of points shown for the section where your line stops.

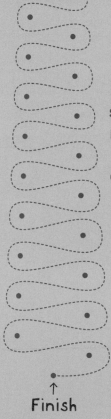

15-24 points · 25-34 points · 35-50 points

Dream Vacation

Chill in the mountains.
Hike, ski, and breathe in that fresh air . . . *hmmm.*

OR

Hit the beach.
Catch some waves and build a sandcastle.

Choose one of these two.

Visit a city.
Big buildings, bustling crowds, lots to do? Yes, please!

OR

MOO!

Head to the country.
Enjoy open space filled with cool animals.

What's your perfect vacay?

This chart will help you decide. Choose one of the activities in each pair. Write it down in the next blank space. Keep choosing from each new pair until you have a winner. Once you're done, you can ask your travel buddies what they think, too!

Take a cruise.
Have a splashy vacation on the ocean.

OR

Swing by an amusement park.
Go on as many rides as you can. *Whee!*

Tour a historic spot.
Visit ancient ruins and other incredible landmarks.

OR

Launch into space!
Get closer to the stars with a trip into the galaxy.

46

Still itching to explore? Write down other ideas for dream vacations here:

_____

_____

Fill in the winners.

Say you had a time machine. Where would you go?

1 I'd visit the dinosaurs, obviously.

2 Methinks the Renaissance would be grand.

3 Beam me to the future, please.

4 Ancient Egypt, here I come.

5 A trip to see the Vikings would be cool.

6 Or jot down your own idea here:

_____

THE FINAL TWO

MY VACATION CHOICE:

EXPRESS YOURSELF

Draw What You See

What do you see out the window? Use a pencil, pen, crayon, or marker to sketch the scene. (If the scenery is moving by too quickly, try taking a picture of the view from the window. Then sketch out the scene captured in the photo.)

Write a Vacation Theme Song

What are some of the highlights of your trip? Here's how you can write a song about them.

1. Choose a simple tune, such as "My Country 'Tis of Thee," "Frère Jacques," "B-i-n-g-o," or "Row, Row, Row Your Boat."

2. Think of words that help describe your trip's highlights. Write them down.

3. Now think of words that rhyme or nearly rhyme with the words you wrote in step 2. Write these down.

4. Come up with phrases that contain the words you listed. Make sure the phrases fit with the tune you chose in step 1. We've given some examples to get you started!

OUR TRIP
[SUNG TO THE TUNE OF "MY COUNTRY 'TIS OF THEE"]

Our trip, it is a blast
In water we do splash,
With wrinkle-y skin.
We came here in a car,
It wasn't very far,
Not sure-ure where we are—
Who's got the map?

THE BEACH

[SUNG TO THE TUNE OF
"FRÈRE JACQUES"]

Our vacation, our vacation.

So much fun! So much fun!

Sand and sun and ice cream.

Insect bites and sunscreen.

We'll be back. We'll be back.

THE CAR

[SUNG TO THE TUNE OF
"ROW, ROW, ROW YOUR BOAT"]

Pack, squeeze, jam the car

With all our many things.

Most of them will not be used,

A family trip begins!

51

Create a Comic

Create a comic based on an adventure you had on your trip. First, jot down characters to include, story notes, and a title. Then divide the adventure into a series of scenes and sketch them in the blank spaces.

CHARACTER LIST

STORY NOTES

TITLE:

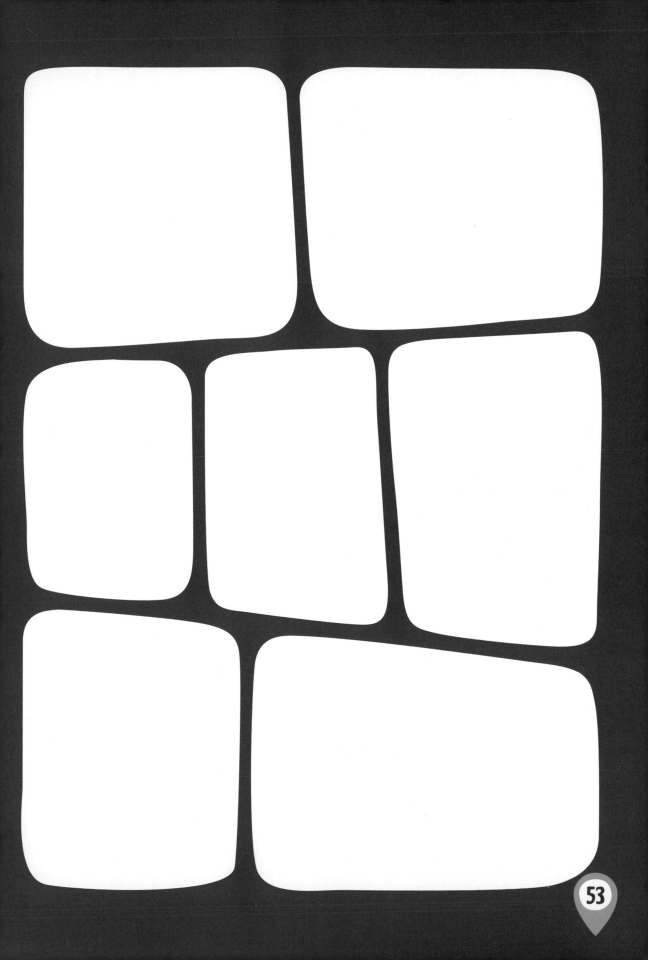

Write a Poem

One way to express your thoughts and feelings is through poetry. There are many different types of poems. Here are two forms to get you started: rhyming poems and haikus. Read about them, then write your own poems on the next page!

Rhyming Poems . . .

can be about any topic. You can keep things simple by making your poem four lines and rhyming every other line or the first two lines and the last two lines. Try to give your rhyming lines the same number of syllables. Here are two examples:

MOUNTAIN HIKE

Panting, panting, we're out on a hike.
Panting, panting, wish I had my bike.
Twenty yards more, the peak's within reach.
Maybe next time we'll go to the beach.

TAKING FLIGHT

I love it when the plane takes off
And zooms up into the sky.
We see the tiny world below,
And watch the clouds roll on by.

Haikus . . .

are often about what you observe in your surroundings. These poems have three lines: five syllables in the first line, seven syllables in the second line, and five syllables in the last line. Here are two examples:

THE LAKE

Canoe glides softly,
Smells of summer, insects buzz.
My favorite place.

BASEBALL

Out at the ballpark,
Greenest of grass, blazing sun.
Home run for my team.

54

Dot to Dot

Connecting dots can help you practice your drawing skills. Connect the dots from 1 to 30 to see something that goes at the end of a train.

Make Your Own Connect the Dots!

Sketch the outline of an object. It can be an airplane, lighthouse, tree—whatever. Using a pen, add dots along the outline. (Make sure to space out the dots.) Number the dots to show the order in which they should get connected. Erase the pencil lines in between the dots, then give your puzzle to a travel buddy to complete.

Untangle a Tale

This story-starter maze gives you 25 different story ideas.
Try a few, then create a story below using your favorite one.

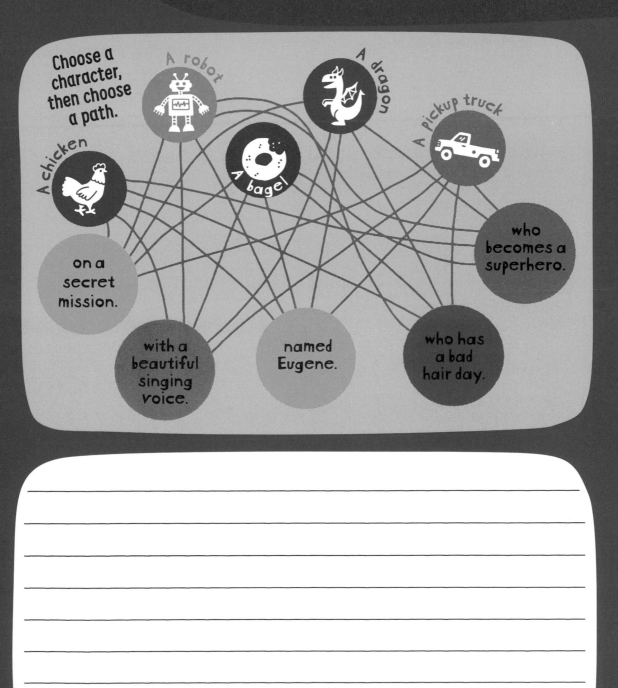

Choose a character, then choose a path.

A robot

A dragon

A pickup truck

A chicken

A bagel

on a secret mission.

who becomes a superhero.

with a beautiful singing voice.

named Eugene.

who has a bad hair day.

Wild Drawings

Learn to draw different animals!

Draw a Bear

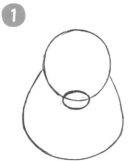

BONUS
MAKE UP A
STORY ABOUT
THE BEAR YOU
DREW. WHY
IS IT SO
GRUMPY?

_____
_____
_____
_____
_____
_____
_____

Draw a Monkey

Draw a Penguin

Use This Space!

What are you feeling *right* now? Draw, doodle, or write out these feelings in the space below.

Hide It!

Can you hide a golf club, like the one below, in a drawing? We gave you a few ideas.

Write a Thank-You Note

Sending a letter is a great way to brighten a person's day. Write a thank-you note to someone who did a kind thing for you on your trip. You can draft your note on the next page, and then rewrite the note on a separate piece of paper and mail it. Your letter doesn't have to be long—it just needs a few words to explain why you are thankful. You can also tell a bit more about your trip and send the person you're writing warm wishes. Here's an example.

Dear Aunt Layla,

Thank you for making our trip to New York City so much fun. I had a great time! My favorite part was seeing the Broadway shows. I also loved the eating tour of Chinatown. Yum! After we left the city, we stopped by the beach. It was fun but COLD. And we missed having you there! Hope you are doing well. Thanks again and can't wait for the next time to see you.

Love,
Lily

BRAIN EXERCISES

Mind Maze

Use your noodle to find your way from START to FINISH.

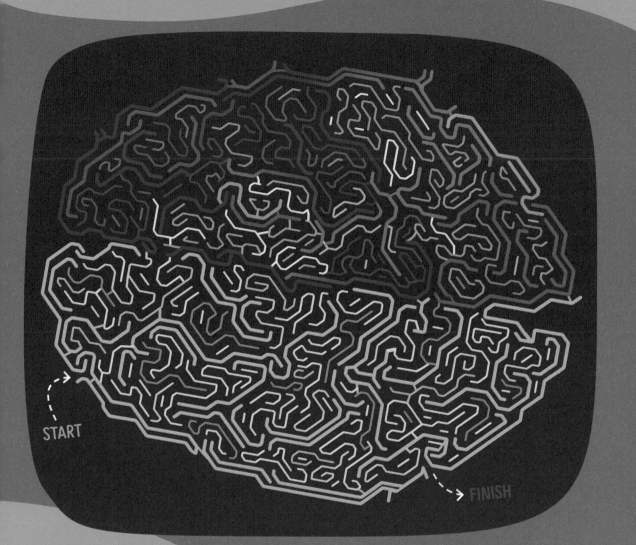

START

FINISH

Trick-Tac-Toe

You know how to play tic-tac-toe. The winner gets three X's or three O's in a row. Trick-tac-toe is played the same way, except the object of the game is the opposite. The loser is the first person who has three X's or three O's in a row.

Brain Boot Camp

Give your brain a workout with these mind-bending challenges! For this activity, you'll need a coin. The first person drops the coin on the tiles and completes the challenge on the tile where the coin lands. Then the next person goes, and so on. Each player has 60 seconds to complete their challenge. Play until you run out of challenges to do.

Count to 90 using multiples of nine.

Write your name with your nondominant hand.

Name as many U.S. states as you can in 60 seconds.

Wink, clap your hands, and then snap your fingers three times in a row.

Recite the first six letters of the alphabet—backward.

Rub your tummy, pat your head, and wiggle your toes all at once.

Read these words: **CAT, FAN, FUN, JAR, CAR**. Now close your eyes and list them in reverse order.

Name five foods that start with the letter *P*.

Say this three times, fast: **Clip, clap, pluck.**

Name five animals that start with the letter *L*.

Come up with three words that each have three syllables.

Tap your foot, pat your elbow, and then blink three times in a row.

Name as many countries as you can in 60 seconds.

Recite the last six letters of the alphabet—backward.

Read these words: **DIG, DOG, LOG, BIG, BAG**. Now close your eyes and list them in reverse order.

Say this three times, fast: **Thin sticks, thick bricks.**

Count to 70 using multiples of seven.

Give your brain a break! Do not complete a challenge this round.

Which letter is missing from the alphabet below? ABCDEFGHIJKLM NOPQRSTUWXYZ

Give a three-sentence description of your day—but make the sentences rhyme.

In a Flash

Try these fast and fun head-scratchers.

Take a Hike

Sticking to the trail is an important part of hiking. Which of the following are real ways to follow a trail?

A A line of cookie crumbs

B A sign on a tree

C A pile of dried corn

D A paint splotch on a tree

E A pile of rocks

Ice Pop Puzzler

Figure out which ice pop should go in place of each question mark so that each column and row contains all four ice pops. Quick, before they melt!

In a Flash

Tic-Tac-Dragon

What do the dragons in each row (vertically, horizontally, and diagonally) have in common?

Luggage Match

Which two suitcases are exactly the same?

Whatever the Weather

What's the weather on your trip? Whatever it is, you can do this puzzle: How many words can you make from the letters in **WEATHER**? We gave you some to get started.

WHAT
_____
EAT
_____

_____
_____
_____
_____
_____
_____
_____
_____

_____
_____
_____
_____
_____
_____
_____
_____
_____

RAIN EXPECTED IN DEW TIME.

WEEKEND FORECAST

LOL!

Would You Rather...

Use these short questions to start some epic conversations with your travel companions.

- Would you rather hang out with a wizard or meet an alien?

- Would you rather sprout wings or grow fins?

- Would you rather be able to talk to animals or read humans' minds?

- Would you rather live on the moon or at the bottom of the sea?

- Would you rather give up chocolate or pizza for a year?

In a Flash

True or False Trivia

What is the one statement below that is **NOT** true?

A The United States has more tornadoes than any other country.

B Snowflakes are actually colorless. They look white because they reflect light.

C Underwater volcanoes spew ice, not lava.

D Baby giraffes are about six feet tall when they're born.

E Whales have belly buttons.

Get Packin'

Unscramble each set of letters to get the name of something you might pack for a trip.

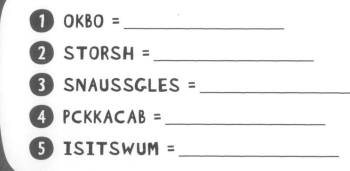

1 OKBO = _____

2 STORSH = _____

3 SNAUSSGLES = _____

4 PCKKACAB = _____

5 ISITSWUM = _____

Buttoned Up

There's only one pair of matching buttons.
Can you find it?

Ride AND Seek

Before you get in line for the ride you want to try first, find at least 25 differences between these two pictures.

Can you find these details in the picture above?

Hidden Pictures Take Two

Each of these scenes contains 12 hidden objects, which are listed on the right. Find each object in one of the scenes, then cross it off the list.

Each object is hidden only once. Can you find them all?

banana
canoe
comb
cupcake
doughnut

envelope
fish
flowerpot
hammer
hot dog

ice-cream cone
ice skate
key
light bulb
mitten

pencil
pennant
slice of pizza
tape dispenser
telescope

toothbrush
waffle
wedge of cheese
yo-yo

Loads of Ladybugs

Can you find the beetle that isn't a ladybug?
Can you also find 12 hidden red ants?

Tricky Stacks

Look closely at the stacks below. Can you figure out how many shipping containers are in each stack?

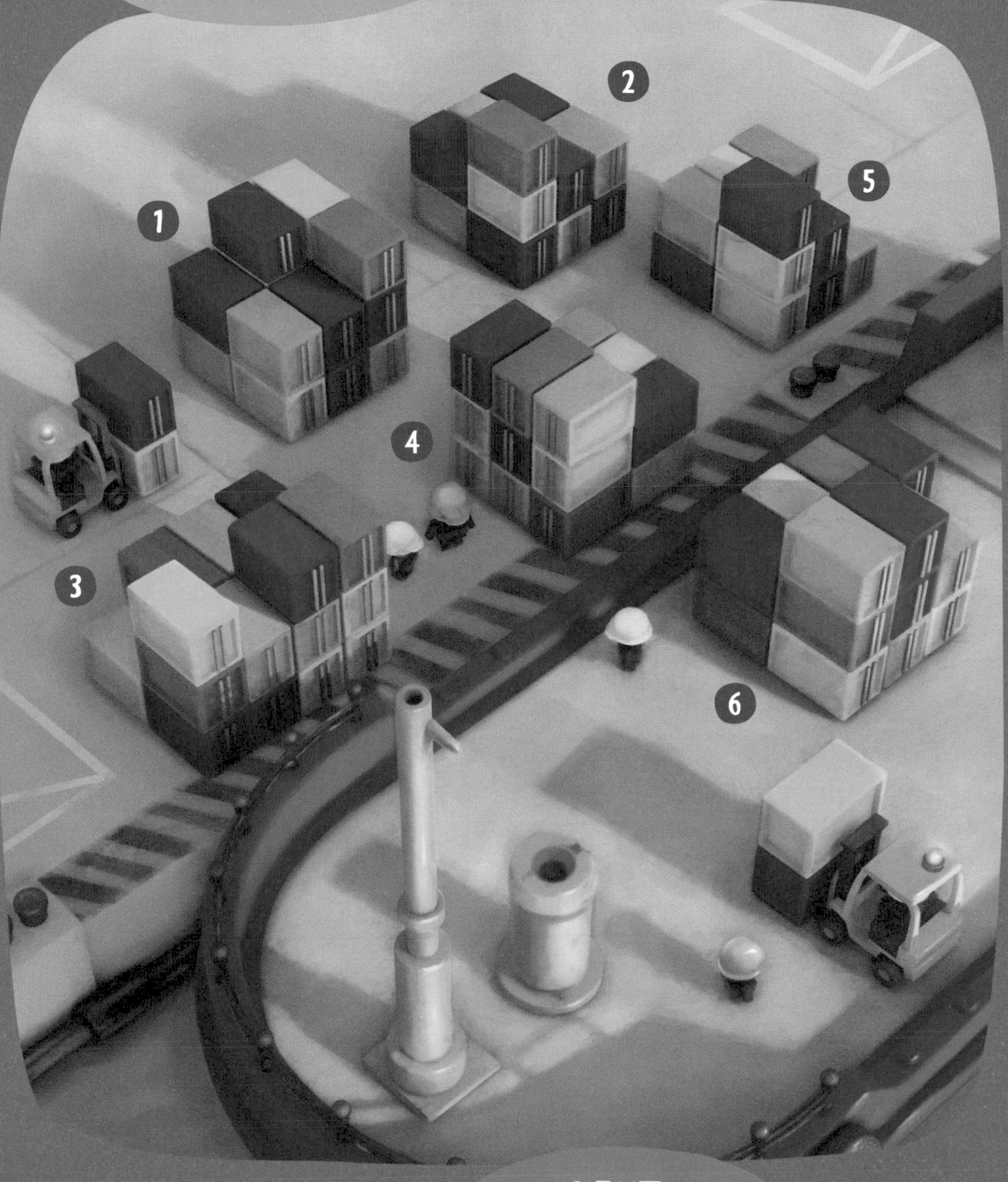

HINT:
SOME CONTAINERS ARE HIDDEN UNDERNEATH OR BEHIND OTHER CONTAINERS.

What Time Is It?

These clocks show the time at the same moment in different parts of the world. Use the times on the clocks to answer the questions below.

SAN FRANCISCO 1 P.M.

NEW YORK 4 P.M.

LONDON 9 P.M.

BERLIN 10 P.M.

ISTANBUL 11 P.M.

If it's 5 a.m. in New York, what time is it in San Francisco? _____

If it's 8 p.m. in Istanbul, what time is it in Berlin? _____

If it's 3 a.m. in London, what time is it in New York? _____

If it's noon in Istanbul, what time is it in London? _____

What is the difference in time between New York and San Francisco? _____

Clock Challenge

These clocks are all wrong! Can you figure out the correct times using the example? Example: 1:89 would be 2:29.

1 2:60

2 8:90

3 4:83

4 11:61

5 5:76

6 7:87

78

What to Pack?

Time to pack for the big trip. But first, you'll have to search through this mess! Can you find everything on your packing list? It includes a pencil, 4 shoes, a banana, a globe, a pair of sunglasses, a truck, 3 yo-yos, a fork, a key, 4 gloves, 2 dinosaurs, 4 books, a jump rope, a clock, an orange sock, and a cactus.

Pet Search

The missing letters in each word or phrase below spell out a type of pet. Cross the words off the list as you fill in each answer. We've fetched the first one for you.

WORD LIST

BIRD	HAMSTER	RABBIT
~~CAT~~	LIZARD	RAT
DOG	MOUSE	SNAKE
FISH	PARROT	TOAD
FROG	PIG	TURTLE

1 Capture something that's in the air

_C_ _A_ _T_CH

2 Icing

__ __ __STIN__

3 Someone who attacks ships at sea

PI__ __ __E

4 Caring only about yourself

SEL__ __ __ __

5 Storm with high winds and snow

B__ __ __Z__ __ __

6 Ate something small between meals

__ __ __C __ __D

7 Date when you were born

__ __ __TH__AY

8 Sleeping

__ __ZIN__

9 Heated bread till it was crispy

__ __ __STE__

10 Gray bird seen in cities

__ __ __EON

11 Long car driven by a chauffeur

LI__ __ __ __IN__

12 Grouchiest

C__ __ __ __ __ES__

13 Man in charge of a private school

__E__D__A__ __ __ __

14 Flap of skin that hangs from a certain bird's neck

__ __ __KEY'S WAT__ __ __

15 Dancers never want to step on this

__ __ __ TNE__'S FO__ __

Sock Scramble

The socks in your suitcase got all mixed up!
Can you find the 8 matching pairs?

Crossword Vacation

Fill in the correct answers using the numbered clues. Hint: If you don't know the answer to a clue, look at the other clues that are around it, both across and down, or try another part of the puzzle and come back to the tough clue later.

ACROSS

1 Commercials

4 Fog; rhymes with *daze*

8 Signal from a ship in trouble

11 "Skip to My ____ , My Darlin' "

12 You screw this onto a jar (2 words)

13 Fuzz in one's belly button or in the dryer

14 Summer vacation activity in a pool, a lake, or an ocean

16 China's continent

17 "Hold ____ ____ your hat!" (2 words)

18 Summer vacation activity with a tent

20 How chic!: "____ la la!"

23 Rodent in a lab

24 Cloth for cleaning; rhymes with *tag*

27 Religious woman who lives in a convent

29 Outfits worn by the ancient Romans

33 Place with rides that you visit during summer vacation (2 words)

36 Another word for *mothers*

37 One of five on your foot

38 Messy place a pig calls home

39 ____ Willie Winkie

41 They perform checkups (abbreviation)

43 Vacation transportation (two-wheeled)

47 " ____ upon a time . . ."

51 Not busy; rhymes with *bridle*

52 Summer vacation activity that you play with a bat

55 Close by

56 Kitchen appliance you use for baking

57 Negative answers; opposite of *yeses*

58 What beavers build

59 Unwanted plant in a garden

60 Our closest primate

DOWN

1 "One more thing . . ."

2 One of two directions in a crossword puzzle

3 Business outfit

4 *Green Eggs and ____*

5 ____ *Baba and the Forty Thieves*

6 ____ oxide (sunscreen compound)

7 Mystery writer ____ Allan Poe

8 "Yes, yes" in Spanish (2 words)

9 "The door's open. Come ____ ____ !" (2 words)

10 Male deer

13 Portable computer

15 Cow's sound

19 "Never mind. It doesn't ____ ."

21 "I'll be there in ____ ____ ." (immediately; 2 words)

22 Low, buzzing sound; rhymes with *gum*

24 Male sheep

25 I ____ ____ child (2 words)

26 Bubble ____

28 Hit the tennis ball over the ____

30 "Food" for cars

31 Drawing or painting class

32 Cloud's home

34 *Tom ____* (Mark Twain novel; rhymes with *lawyer*)

35 Head movement for a yes response

40 Bendable part of the arm

42 Cry uncontrollably

43 In a ____ (stuck)

44 A thought

45 Seafood often served in chowder

46 Roof overhang

48 Nickname for grandma

49 Sound of a hoof on pavement: clip ____

50 "Would you like anything ____?"

53 Look at; observe

54 Finish

1 2 3 4 5 6 7 8 9 10
11 12 13
14 15 16
17 18 19
20 21 22 23
24 25 26 27 28 29 30 31 32
33 34 35
36 37 38
39 40 41 42
WEE
43 44 45 46 47 48 49 50
51 52 53 54
55 56 57
58 59 60

Beading Frenzy

In these beads, there are 10 hidden items. Can you find the cupcake, balloon, lime, lollipop, button, heart, cherries, fish, umbrella, and apple?

Coral Confusion

Dive into this coral maze. Can you find a path from START to FINISH?

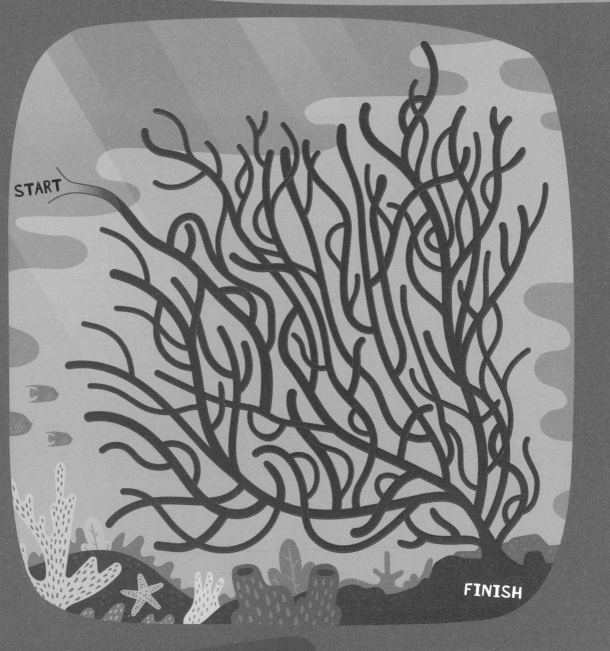

Fun Facts

- Some types of coral can make their own light.
- Coral have growth rings, like trees.
- Around 6,000 species of coral exist around the world.

85

The Great State Search

All 50 states are hiding in this USA-shaped word search. They are hidden forward, backward, up, down, and diagonally. We circled one to get you started.

```
        I
    N D N O S H U
    O E N E W H A M P S H I R E
    R L B A V A T W Y O M I N G A R K A N S A S
  N T A K R M A S S A C H U S E T T S X F Z Q X
  O H W H I A M D Q O I M E T O S X A N A T N O M N
  T C A N Z L S O A I U I A H X C A L I F O R N I A
  G A R Q O A R K S A L T A R X M I C H I G A N S E
W N R E Q N B S L A L F D H Y Y W N E W J E R S E Y
W I O Z J A A O A G M I L N C O L O R A D O R K G O
U H L D E X M M H O B U O O V A V A X D F R G F C S
S S I U E W A C O V X G A V R K R L N P P G I A A A
A A N T M Q F T M N E W M E X I C O U D E I A K I T
  W A N U T A H A R G Y I R S L D P L U T A W E A O
  N E W Y O R K O E N I A M W O X A G I P B P M R K
    A I N I G R I V F L O Z U V M D Q N S U O S A
    R H O D E I S L A N D I A K S A L A F E Z D
      M I N N E S O T A S N X T G Y I N F S H
      J H I P P I S S I S S I M L N R N S T
        Q H K D Y A E E S S E N N E T U
            C O N N E C T I C U T F O
            B A Q M I S S O U R I S
              O H I O O
              T W Z S
              C U H
              H
```

WORD LIST

~~ALABAMA~~	MONTANA
ALASKA	NEBRASKA
ARIZONA	NEVADA
ARKANSAS	NEW HAMPSHIRE
CALIFORNIA	NEW JERSEY
COLORADO	NEW MEXICO
CONNECTICUT	NEW YORK
DELAWARE	NORTH CAROLINA
FLORIDA	NORTH DAKOTA
GEORGIA	OHIO
HAWAII	OKLAHOMA
IDAHO	OREGON
ILLINOIS	PENNSYLVANIA
INDIANA	RHODE ISLAND
IOWA	SOUTH CAROLINA
KANSAS	SOUTH DAKOTA
KENTUCKY	TENNESSEE
LOUISIANA	TEXAS
MAINE	UTAH
MARYLAND	VERMONT
MASSACHUSETTS	VIRGINIA
MICHIGAN	WASHINGTON
MINNESOTA	WEST VIRGINIA
MISSISSIPPI	WISCONSIN
MISSOURI	WYOMING

THE GREAT OUTDOORS

Bird Sudoku

Write each bird's name in the squares so that the six kinds of birds appear only once in each row, column, and 2 × 3 box.

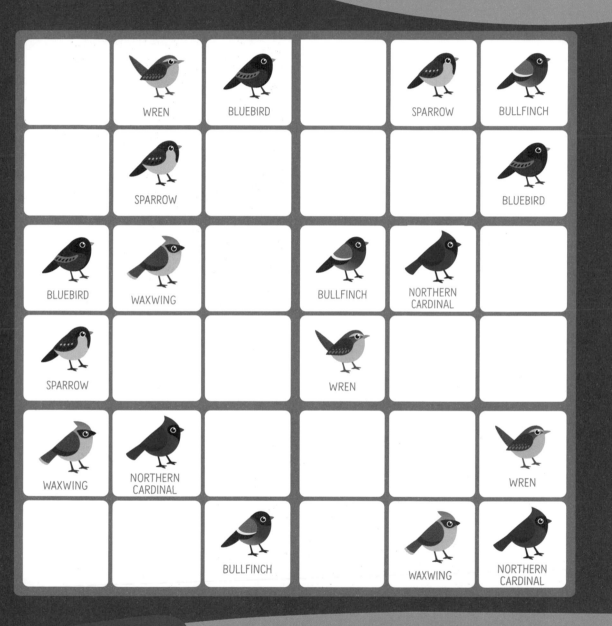

Birding Tips

Wherever you travel, you'll likely spot cool birds. Here are tips for observing them.

- It can be easier to hear a bird than to see one. Close your eyes and listen for bird calls. Then look in the direction where the sounds are coming from.
- Draw the birds you see. If you're unsure of the type of bird you've spotted, look it up and label your drawing. This will help you get to know different bird species.
- Many bird species are most active early in the day, so morning is often the best time to observe birds.

6 by SIX

Each of these outdoorsy scenes contains 6 hidden objects from the list below. Some objects are hidden in more than one scene. Can you find the 6 hidden objects in each scene?

HIDDEN OBJECT LIST

ARTIST'S BRUSH (2)	HOCKEY STICK (2)
BANANA (3)	LIGHTNING BOLT (2)
BOOMERANG (2)	LOLLIPOP (3)
BROCCOLI (3)	MITTEN (5)
COMB (3)	PAPER CLIP (3)
CROWN (4)	PENCIL (4)

BONUS
TWO SCENES CONTAIN THE EXACT SAME SET OF HIDDEN OBJECTS. CAN YOU FIND THAT MATCHING PAIR?

Forest Match

Hidden Words

It's smooth sailing for this family! There are six words (not pictures!) hidden in the scene below. Can you find BOAT, FISH, LAND, MOM, WATER, and WIND?

Speaking of Sailing . . .

Say each tongue twister three times, fast.

FISH SCALES— SHINING, SILVERY!

WIND WHIPS OVER THE WATER.

OUR BLUE BOAT IS BETTER IN THIS WEATHER.

Comics Mix-Up

These cartoons are missing something—speech balloons! Can you match each speech balloon to the correct comic?

A WELL, THIS IS EMBARRASSING—YOU'D THINK I'D KNOW HOW TO TWEET!

B MY NAME IS ALSO TEDDY!

C THAT'S WEIRD— MY LIGHTER'S NOT WORKING EITHER! ANYONE HAVE A MATCH?

D WE'RE GETTING TOO CLOSE TO THE CITY. I'M PICKING UP A CELL PHONE CONVERSATION!

95

States of Wonder

Check out awesome natural marvels in two U.S. states: Utah and Florida.

Arches Galore!

Utah boasts some eye-popping places, including Arches National Park. Put the names of these Utah hot spots into the crisscross puzzle below. Each word fits into the grid in only one way. Use the number of letters in each word as a clue to where it might fit.

WORD LIST

4 LETTERS
ZION

5 LETTERS
DIXIE
OURAY

6 LETTERS
ARCHES

8 LETTERS
DINOSAUR

10 LETTERS
GLEN CANYON
MANTI-LA SAL

11 LETTERS
CANYONLANDS
CAPITOL REEF
CEDAR BREAKS

12 LETTERS
FLAMING GORGE
GOBLIN VALLEY

ARCHES NATIONAL PARK HAS OVER 2,000 NATURAL ARCHES. THE DELICATE ARCH IS FEATURED ON UTAH LICENSE PLATES.

Winding Wetlands

Everglades National Park in Florida is home to one of the largest wetlands in the world. Find the one path from **START** to **FINISH** in this wetlands maze. Then use the letters along the correct path to spell out a furry Everglades animal.

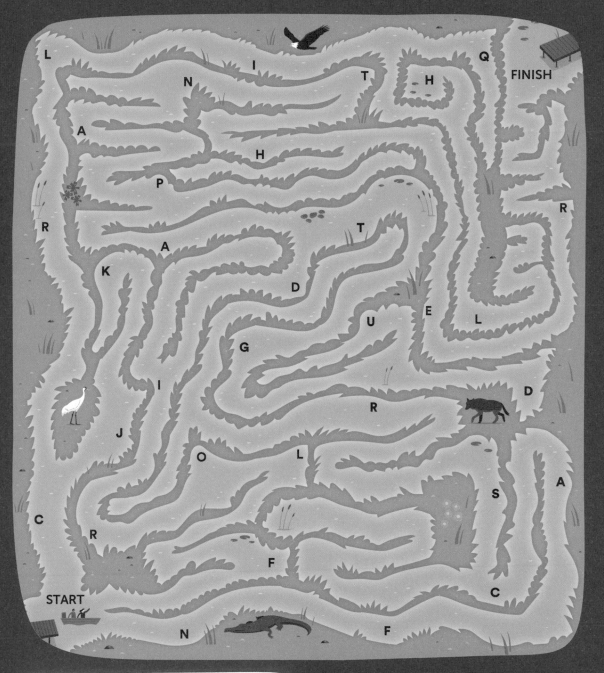

_____ _____ _____ _____ _____

WETLANDS ARE
COMPLEX HABITATS THAT
INCLUDE MARSHES, SWAMPS,
BOGS, AND LAGOONS.

Creepy Crawly Quiz

This quiz looks like a job for an insect expert. Read each sentence below and circle T if you think it's true and F if you think it's false.

T F **1** Insects have been around for more than 400 million years, even before the dinosaurs.

T F **2** Three types of dragonfly can breathe fire.

T F **3** All ladybugs are female.

T F **4** Even other insects think that cockroaches are gross.

T F **5** In warmer weather, crickets chirp faster.

T F **6** It takes one year for a centipede to cross all of its legs.

T F **7** Houseflies live for only one month.

T F **8** Some swarms of cicadas are louder than a rock concert.

T F **9** Stinkbugs can only hang out together if they wear nose plugs.

T F **10** The praying mantis is the only insect that can turn its head.

T F **11** Spiders have eight legs, which means they're not insects.

T F **12** Bees are the only insects that produce food that humans eat—honey.

T F **13** Ants can carry 10 to 50 times their body weight.

T F **14** Fireflies require two AAA batteries.

T F **15** A ladybug's spots fade as it gets older.

T F **16** The venom in a black widow spider is 15 times stronger than a rattlesnake's venom.

Nature Close-Up

How many of these zoomed-in photos from nature can you identify?

1

2

3

4

5

6

7

8

Ant's Journey

This tiny traveler needs help making it home. Use the branches to find a path from START to FINISH.

START

FINISH

BONUS
ONCE YOU FIND THE RIGHT PATH
WRITE DOWN THE LETTERS YOU PASS
ALONG THE WAY TO ANSWER THE RIDDLE
WHAT IS THE BIGGEST ANT IN THE WORLD?

Polar Patterns

Find each pattern in the grid below.

1

2

3

4

5

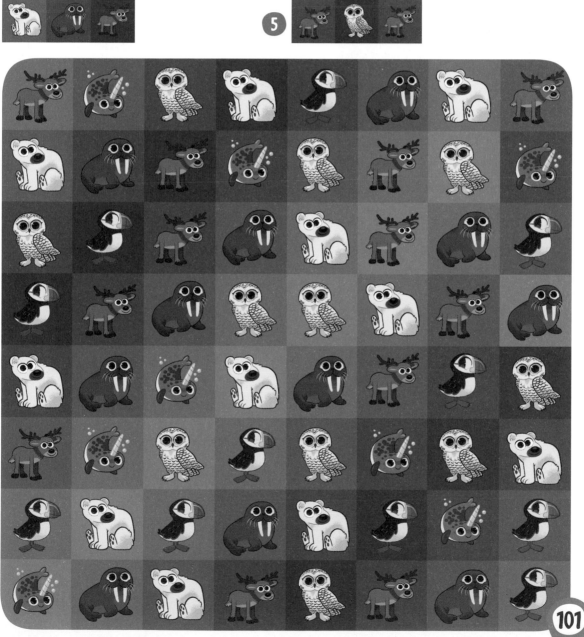

Who Knows the Nose?

Can you identify each animal by its nose alone? If you get five or more correct answers, give yourself a pat on the back (and a scratch behind your ears)!

Awesome Blossoms

Find 4 shamrocks, 4 butterflies, 6 dragonflies, and a purple beetle.

103

ROAD
FOOD

Dinner Scramble

This furry chef whipped up some delicious food for hungry, dog-tired travelers. But he scrambled the menu, so you must sit, stay, and solve before eating. Unscramble each food item, then put the numbered letters in the correct spaces below to answer the riddle.

OPUS   __ __ __ __
           15

COAT   __ __ __ __
              3

WEST   __ __ __ __
       4

TAKES   __ __ __ __ __
        11

HILIC   __ __ __ __ __
           6

LADSA   __ __ __ __ __
      1

REGRUB   __ __ __ __ __ __
    2

RIST YFR   __ __ __ __   __ __ __
      5   9

FLEAMOAT   __ __ __ __ __ __ __ __
          8

TAGHPESIT   __ __ __ __ __ __ __ __ __
        14   12

HIFS KISSCT   __ __ __ __   __ __ __ __ __
     10   13

POSPLY SOJE   __ __ __ __ __ __   __ __ __
       16   7

WHAT DID THE DOG SERVE WITH DINNER?

__   __ __ __ __ __ __   __ __
1   2   3   4   5   6   7   8   9

__ __ __ __ __ - __ __.
10   11   12   13   14   15   16

Pairs of Pies

Each pizza has an exact match—except one. Can you find the one without a match?

Crisscross Cone

What makes any vacation even better? Ice-cream! Fill in the crisscross with the ice-cream flavors and toppings from the word list. Use the number of letters in each word as a clue to where it fits.

WORD LIST

4 LETTERS
MINT

6 LETTERS
CHERRY

7 LETTERS
VANILLA

8 LETTERS
HOT FUDGE

9 LETTERS
CHOCOLATE
ROCKY ROAD
SPRINKLES

11 LETTERS
BANANA SPLIT
COOKIE DOUGH

12 LETTERS
WHIPPED CREAM

Fruit-tastic Fun!

Can you find the right path through the fruit? The symbols tell you which way to move.

 Move 1 space **DOWN**
 Move 1 space **LEFT**
 Move 1 space **RIGHT**
STOP

Path 1 Path 2 Path 3 Path 4 Path 5 Path 6

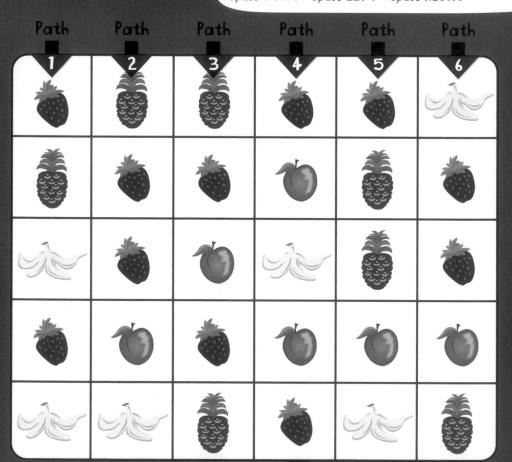

exit

Juicy Jokes

WHAT'S A VAMPIRE'S FAVORITE FRUIT?
A blood orange.

WHAT DO YOU CALL SAD STRAWBERRIES?
Blueberries.

WHAT DO YOU GIVE A SICK LEMON?
Lemon aid.

Tic-Tac-Taco

What do the tacos in each row (horizontally, vertically, and diagonally) have in common?

Jelly Bean Jigsaw

Can you find these seven jigsaw pieces in the photo of jelly beans?

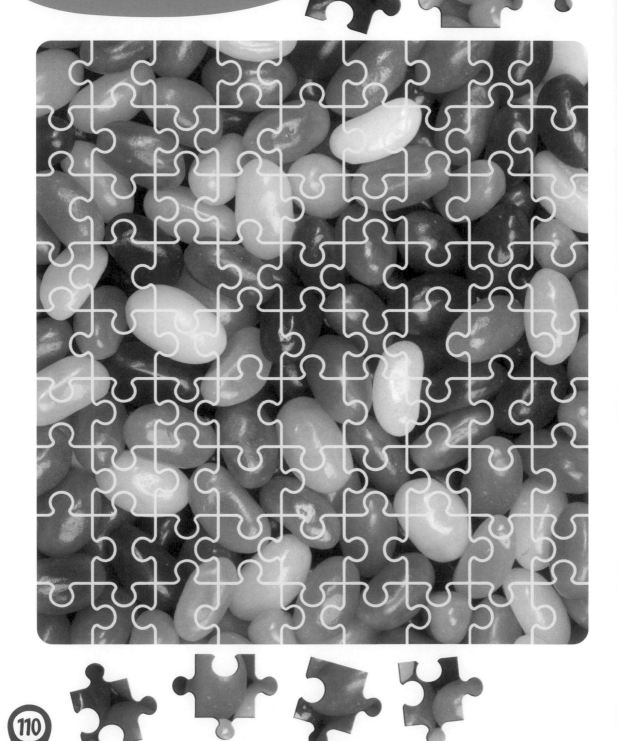

Breakfast of Champions

Draw your idea of a perfect breakfast.

Undersea Eatery

How many matching pairs of creatures can you find at this underwater diner?

HOOKS

DINER

LANDFOOD

SEAFOOD

WE'RE OPEN

What's Wrong?

This alien diner is out of this world. What wacky things do you see? It's up to you!

OUR MOONCAKES ARE OUT OF THIS WORLD!

Moonbeam DINER

SPECIALS
GALAXY MELT
METEOR MASH

CHARGING STATION

Sprinkles, Please

These sprinkles are hiding 19 crayons.
Can you find them all?

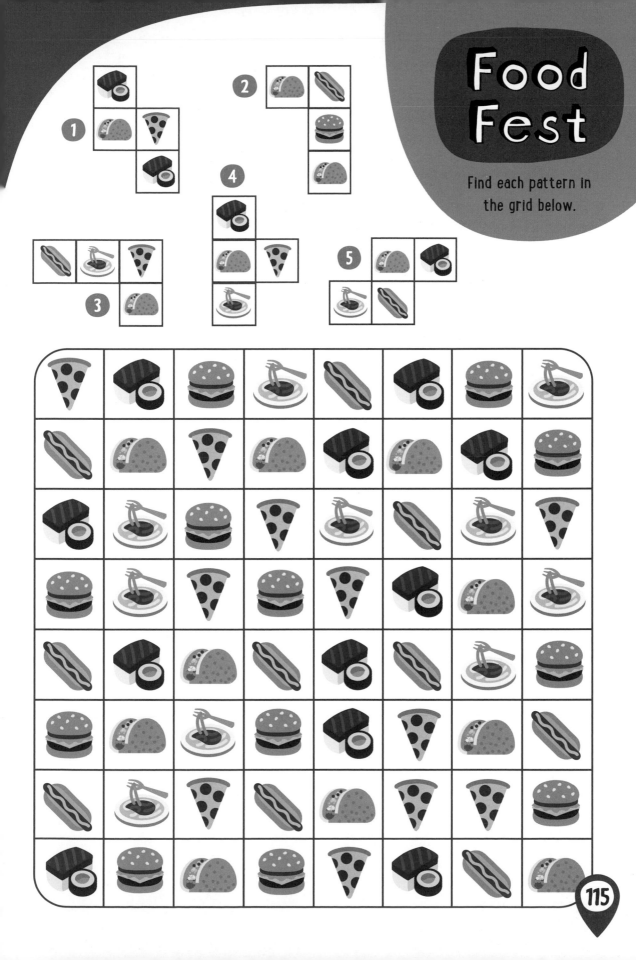

Food Fest

Find each pattern in the grid below.

SPACE TRAVEL

Meet Your Tour Guide!

One of these aliens is your tour guide to the galaxy. Find the alien who:

- has more than two ears
- is holding a snack
- doesn't have a hat or crown
- doesn't have purple hair
- has tentacles
- has fewer than four eyes

BONUS
PLAY THIS GAME WITH A TRAVEL BUDDY. CHOOSE AN ALIEN WITHOUT TELLING THEM WHICH ONE YOU'VE CHOSEN. YOUR TRAVEL BUDDY ASKS YES OR NO QUESTIONS ABOUT THE ALIEN UNTIL THEY CAN GUESS WHICH ONE YOU'VE CHOSEN. TAKE TURNS CHOOSING AND GUESSING.

Astro Adventure

Find your way through the Imagination Constellations from **START** to **FINISH**. Be sure to avoid the satellites along the way. Then solve the word puzzles.

START

Are there more blue (hotter) stars or red (cooler) stars?

RIDDLE 1:
When will pigs fly into space?

RIDDLE 2:
How do you get a baby astronaut to fall asleep?

RIDDLE 3:
Why did the moon stop eating?

RIDDLE 4:
What do astronauts eat for breakfast?

FINISH

Unscramble this word to find out what kind of puzzle solver you are.

L A R S T E L !

_____

Home Sweet Home

Zig, Vot, and Spo are homesick. Can you use the clues to match each alien with the right spaceship and home planet? Use the chart to keep track of your answers. Put an X in each box that can't be true and an O in boxes that match.

	Hot Planet	Cold Planet	Wet Planet	Red Ship	Yellow Ship	Blue Ship
Zig						
Vot						
Spo						

CLUES:
1. The red spaceship came from a hot planet.
2. Vot's planet is cold, but not wet.
3. The yellow spaceship belongs to Spo.

Rocket Ship Word Search

Inside this rocket are 34 space terms.
Can you find them all?

WORD LIST

APOGEE
ARMS
ASTRONAUTS
ATOMIC
BOOSTERS
CAPE CANAVERAL
CAPSULES
CARGO
CELESTIAL
CONTROL
COSMOS
FAIL-SAFE
FORCE
FUNDED
GUIDANCE SYSTEMS
LANDER
MANNED SPACESHIP
MISSION
MOMENTUM
MOONS
MOUNTAIN
NECK-WRENCHING
  G-FORCES
NOSE CONE
ORBIT
PERIGEE
RAMJET
RANGER
REENTRY
SALVO
SPLASHDOWN
SPACE DEBRIS
THRUSTER
ZERO
ZOOM

Space Quiz

See how stellar your knowledge of space is with this quiz.

1 Pluto is known as this.
  A. A dwarf planet
  B. A baby planet
  C. A puppy planet

2 Which planet is closest to the sun?
  A. Earth
  B. Venus
  C. Mercury

3 How much bigger is the sun's diameter than that of Earth's?
  A. 19 times bigger
  B. 109 times bigger
  C. 19 million times bigger

4 What are Saturn's rings made up of?
  A. Fiery gas
  B. Gold and diamonds
  C. Ice, dust, and rocks

5 What is a common nickname for Mars?
  A. The Red Planet
  B. The Green Planet
  C. E.T.'s Home Planet

6 What year did astronauts first walk on the moon?
  A. 1949
  B. 1969
  C. 1999

Space Travel Fast Facts

1 All food packages in space use Velcro so the food doesn't float away.

2 A space suit weighs approximately 280 pounds on Earth—but when it's in space, it's weightless.

3 Foods such as cookies and bread aren't allowed in space because the crumbs can get stuck in important equipment.

4 When astronauts return from space, they often drop things because they're so used to an environment with zero gravity.

121

Race Through Space

Your mission: Race your fellow astronauts to Planet Zipzop. Read the directions below to get started. 3, 2, 1, blastoff!

TO PLAY:

1 Tear out a game piece for each player and numbers 1 to 5 from page 143. Place the game pieces on START. Put the numbers in a hat, empty bag, or other container.

2 When it's your turn, close your eyes and pick a number from the container. Then move your piece that number of spaces. Follow the directions on the space where you land.

3 The first player to reach FINISH wins!

FOR 2 TO 4 PLAYERS

START

You've finally launched into space! Come up with a short cheer to show your excitement.

Oh dear, someone forgot the map! Go back to START.

Your spacecraft went into hyperdrive—move ahead two spaces.

Is that your tummy rumbling? Make a pitstop at a space diner. Miss your next turn.

You pass a ship of Gorkin aliens. Give them a Gorkin wave to say hello.

Time to unpack! Name **three** items you can't live without on long trips from home.

Whoa—you just passed a never-before-seen moon! Give it a name.

You found a shortcut around the Yippy Asteroid. Move ahead **one** space.

Even astronauts must brush their teeth! Act out brushing your chompers in space.

WHO WILL GET TO PLANET ZIPZOP FIRST?

FINISH

Almost there! Make up a short poem about Zipzop to share with Zipzopians.

Oops! Someone accidentally put the spacecraft in reverse. Move back three spaces.

To greet one another, Bogo aliens wink, snap, and then say, "Wah, wah, wah." Greet someone the Bogo way!

You have to stop for more rocket fuel. Miss your next turn.

Ground control sent a message. Say it aloud three times, fast: Shiny, shimmery, silver stars.

You were just awarded Best Astronaut Ever. Give a brief acceptance speech.

You've decided to write a book about your travels to Zipzop. What's the book's title?

Someone spilled their drink—and the liquid is floating everywhere. Act out cleaning up this space mess.

Feeling antsy? Come up with a sport to play on your spacecraft. What are the rules?

A faster spacecraft has offered to tow you. Move ahead two spaces.

Your crew is making good time! Do an astronaut victory dance from your seat.

Uh oh—a star exploded! Move back one space to keep a safe distance.

Make a space swap! Switch places on the board with another player.

Grumpy Floofah aliens are flying by. Freeze in place for 30 seconds so they won't notice you.

Cosmic Code

In the messages, each of the letters has been replaced by a random number. Use the key to fill in some of the letters. Then use the hints to figure out the letters that are missing from the key.

13 10 9 9 5 ,
13 10 9 9 5 ,
13 10 9 9 5 !

4 26 12 18 ,
13 2 21 10 24 12 13 2 6
4 20 10 2 3 15 2 25 12
23 10 12 .

20 5 2 25 12 18 24 1 -
19 2 20 12 18 2 24
19 2 9 9 5 8 25 .

Time to get ready for launch!

What are those sticks for?

What do you think of my cool spaceship?

18 12 25 5 26 12 5 15 ,
12 13 18 25 8 5 20 9 6 !

HINTS
18 is either A or I.
12 is either G or T.
9 is either L or X.
25 is either S or Z.

KEY

1	2	3	4	5	6	7	8	9	10	11	12	13	14	15	16	17	18	19	20	21	22	23	24	25	26
	K	B	O	D	Q	W			E	C		H	P	F	X	Z		M	R	V	J	Y	N		U

Tic Tac Planet

What do the planets in each row (horizontally, vertically, and diagonally) have in common?

Speaking of Space . . .

HOW DID MARY'S LITTLE LAMB GET TO MARS?
By rocket sheep.

HOW DO YOU KNOW WHEN THE MOON IS BROKE?
When it's down to its last quarter.

HOW IS FOOD SERVED IN SPACE?
On satellite dishes.

Comics Mix-Up

These cartoons are missing something—speech balloons! Can you match each speech balloon to the correct comic?

What's Wrong?

What things in this picture are silly? It's up to you!

Space Puzzler

We're blasting off to outer space, but we forgot to pack our vowels! Can you figure out each of these space-related words?

1. ECLPS = _ _ _ _ _ _ _
2. JPTR = _ _ _ _ _ _ _
3. PLNT = _ _ _ _ _ _
4. GLXY = _ _ _ _ _ _
5. STRN = _ _ _ _ _ _
6. BLCK HL = _ _ _ _ _ _ _ _ _ _
7. SLR FLR = _ _ _ _ _ _ _ _ _ _
8. SLR SYSTM = _ _ _ _ _ _ _ _ _ _ _
9. CMT = _ _ _ _ _
10. BG DPPR = _ _ _ _ _ _ _ _

WRITE THE HIGHLIGHTED LETTERS IN ORDER ON THE SPACES BELOW TO SOLVE THE RIDDLE.

HOW DOES THE SOLAR SYSTEM TELL JOKES?

With a lot of

_ _ _ _ _ _ _ _ _ _ _ _

Without clues or knowing what things to look for, can you find 13 hidden objects?

Tune-up Spot

Time for a super silly space story! First look for the 12 hidden objects in the picture. Write down each item in the blank spaces of the story as you find them. Once you've found all the objects and the story is filled in, read the story aloud for a laugh.

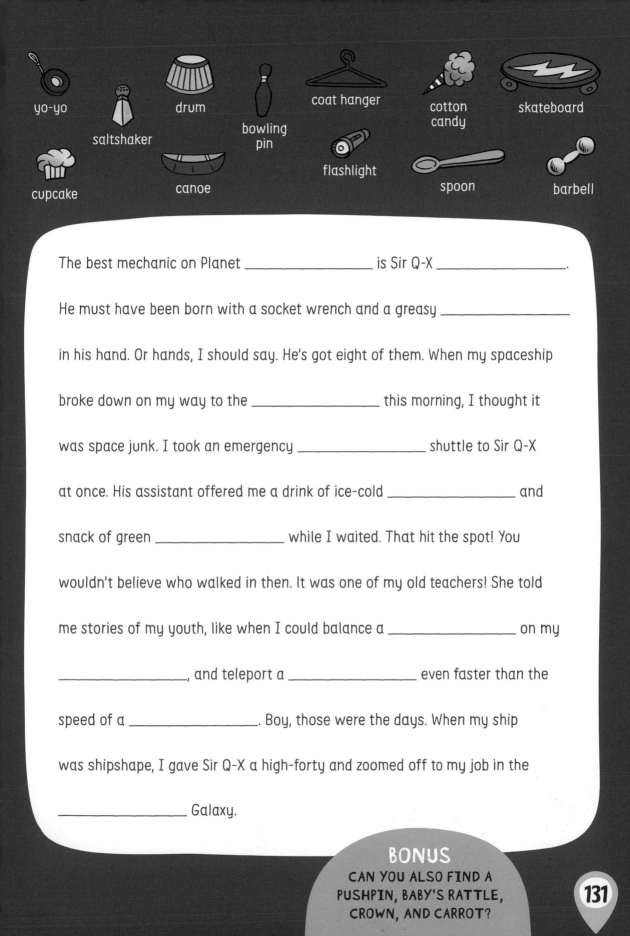

yo-yo

saltshaker

drum

bowling pin

coat hanger

flashlight

cotton candy

skateboard

spoon

barbell

cupcake

canoe

The best mechanic on Planet _____ is Sir Q-X _____.

He must have been born with a socket wrench and a greasy _____

in his hand. Or hands, I should say. He's got eight of them. When my spaceship

broke down on my way to the _____ this morning, I thought it

was space junk. I took an emergency _____ shuttle to Sir Q-X

at once. His assistant offered me a drink of ice-cold _____ and

snack of green _____ while I waited. That hit the spot! You

wouldn't believe who walked in then. It was one of my old teachers! She told

me stories of my youth, like when I could balance a _____ on my

_____, and teleport a _____ even faster than the

speed of a _____. Boy, those were the days. When my ship

was shipshape, I gave Sir Q-X a high-forty and zoomed off to my job in the

_____ Galaxy.

BONUS
CAN YOU ALSO FIND A
PUSHPIN, BABY'S RATTLE,
CROWN, AND CARROT?

131

Here Comes the Sun

This puzzle is so bright, you're going to need shades. Circle the 29 words in the grid that contain the word SUN. The word SUN has been replaced with a ☀. Look up, down, across, backward, and diagonally. The uncircled letters answer the trivia question.

WORD LIST

SUNBAKED	SUNDOWN	SUNROOF
SUNBATHE	SUNDRESS	SUNROOM
SUNBEAM	SUNFISH	SUNSCREEN
SUNBLOCK	SUNKEN	SUNSET
SUNBURN	SUNLIGHT	SUNSHINE
SUNBURNED	SUNLIT	SUNSPOT
SUNDAE	SUNNIER	SUNTAN
SUNDAY	SUNNY	TSUNAMI
SUNDECK	SUNRAY	UNSUNG
SUNDIAL	SUNRISE	

TRIVIA QUESTION:

If the sun were the size of a door in your house, how big would Earth be? Put the uncircled letters in order on the blanks.

ANSWER:

____ _____ ____

__ _____.

Far from Home

Help the astronaut find her way back to the spaceship. Collect the letters you pass along the correct way. Put them in the order that you pass them in from START to FINISH, and you'll answer the riddle!

START

FINISH

RIDDLE:

How do you have a good outer-space party?

ANSWER:

_____ ____ ____ - _____.

20
TRAFFIC CHECK

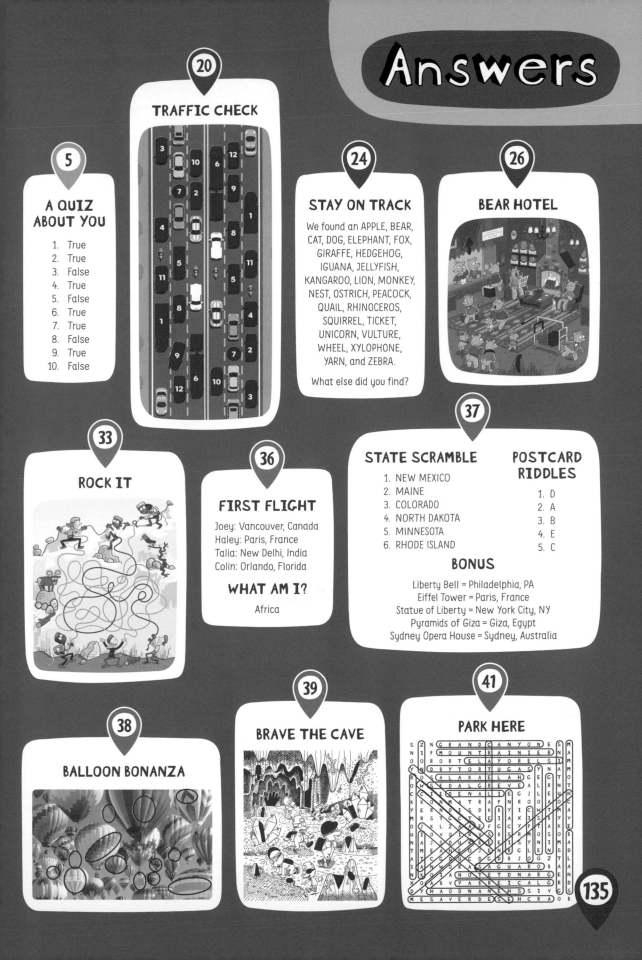

5
A QUIZ ABOUT YOU

1. True
2. True
3. False
4. True
5. False
6. True
7. True
8. False
9. True
10. False

24
STAY ON TRACK

We found an APPLE, BEAR, CAT, DOG, ELEPHANT, FOX, GIRAFFE, HEDGEHOG, IGUANA, JELLYFISH, KANGAROO, LION, MONKEY, NEST, OSTRICH, PEACOCK, QUAIL, RHINOCEROS, SQUIRREL, TICKET, UNICORN, VULTURE, WHEEL, XYLOPHONE, YARN, and ZEBRA.

What else did you find?

26
BEAR HOTEL

33
ROCK IT

36
FIRST FLIGHT

Joey: Vancouver, Canada
Haley: Paris, France
Talia: New Delhi, India
Colin: Orlando, Florida

WHAT AM I?

Africa

37
STATE SCRAMBLE

1. NEW MEXICO
2. MAINE
3. COLORADO
4. NORTH DAKOTA
5. MINNESOTA
6. RHODE ISLAND

POSTCARD RIDDLES

1. D
2. A
3. B
4. E
5. C

BONUS

Liberty Bell = Philadelphia, PA
Eiffel Tower = Paris, France
Statue of Liberty = New York City, NY
Pyramids of Giza = Giza, Egypt
Sydney Opera House = Sydney, Australia

38
BALLOON BONANZA

39
BRAVE THE CAVE

41
PARK HERE

Answers

42

FIRST FLIGHT

1. Emma planned the route.
2. We stopped to sketch at the bridge.
3. Two squirrels came racing along a log!
4. The whole crew ate raisins for energy.
5. We came upon chopped trees near a beaver dam.
6. Our entire crew went slow at challenging, rocky parts of the trail.

BONUS: There are **10** squirrels in the scene.

COMPASS CODE

Where's the best place to eat while hiking?

WHERE THERE'S A FORK IN THE ROAD.

43

TIC TAC CASTLE

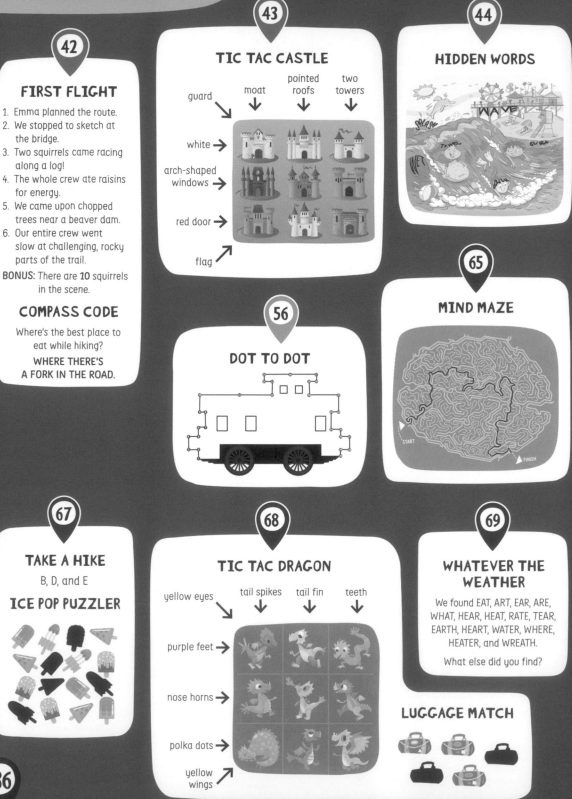

44

HIDDEN WORDS

56

DOT TO DOT

65

MIND MAZE

67

TAKE A HIKE

B, D, and E

ICE POP PUZZLER

68

TIC TAC DRAGON

69

WHATEVER THE WEATHER

We found EAT, ART, EAR, ARE, WHAT, HEAR, HEAT, RATE, TEAR, EARTH, HEART, WATER, WHERE, HEATER, and WREATH.

What else did you find?

LUGGAGE MATCH

Answers

70 TRUE OR FALSE TRIVIA

C is false.

GET PACKIN'
1. Book
2. Shorts
3. Sunglasses
4. Backpack
5. Swimsuit

71 BUTTONED UP

73 RIDE AND SEEK

74 75 HIDDEN PICTURES TAKE TWO

76 LOADS OF LADYBUGS

77 TRICKY STACKS
1. 15
2. 13
3. 18
4. 15
5. 12
6. 16

78 TIME CHANGE
1. 2 a.m.
2. 7 p.m.
3. 10 p.m.
4. 10 a.m.
5. Three hours

CLOCK CHALLENGE
1. 3:00
2. 9:30
3. 5:23
4. 12:01
5. 6:16
6. 8:27

79 WHAT TO PACK?

80 PET SEARCH
1. CATCH (CAT)
2. FROSTING (FROG)
3. PIRATE (RAT)
4. SELFISH (FISH)
5. BLIZZARD (LIZARD)
6. SNACKED (SNAKE)
7. BIRTHDAY (BIRD)
8. DOZING (DOG)
9. TOASTED (TOAD)
10. PIGEON (PIG)
11. LIMOUSINE (MOUSE)
12. CRABBIEST (RABBIT)
13. HEADMASTER (HAMSTER)
14. TURKEY'S WATTLE (TURTLE)
15. PARTNER'S FOOT (PARROT)

 137

Answers

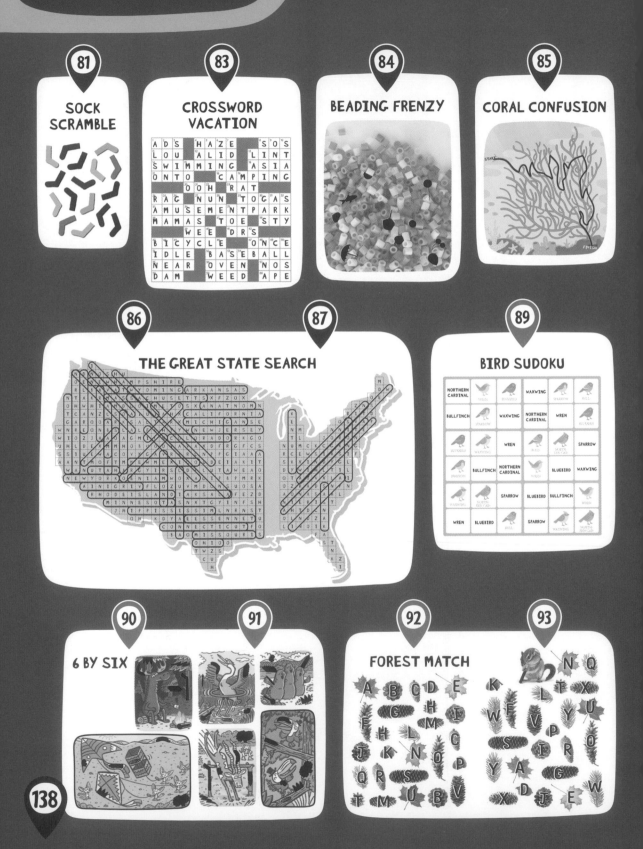

81 SOCK SCRAMBLE

83 CROSSWORD VACATION

84 BEADING FRENZY

85 CORAL CONFUSION

86 87 THE GREAT STATE SEARCH

89 BIRD SUDOKU

90 6 BY SIX

91

92 FOREST MATCH

93

Answers

94
HIDDEN WORDS

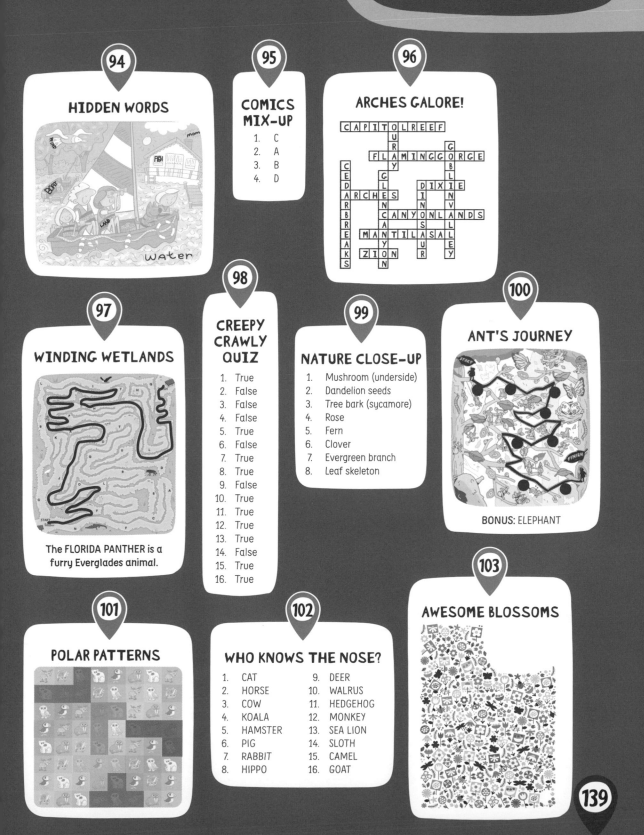

95
COMICS MIX-UP

1. C
2. A
3. B
4. D

96
ARCHES GALORE!

(crossword solution)

97
WINDING WETLANDS

The FLORIDA PANTHER is a furry Everglades animal.

98
CREEPY CRAWLY QUIZ

1. True
2. False
3. False
4. False
5. True
6. False
7. True
8. True
9. False
10. True
11. True
12. True
13. True
14. False
15. True
16. True

99
NATURE CLOSE-UP

1. Mushroom (underside)
2. Dandelion seeds
3. Tree bark (sycamore)
4. Rose
5. Fern
6. Clover
7. Evergreen branch
8. Leaf skeleton

100
ANT'S JOURNEY

BONUS: ELEPHANT

101
POLAR PATTERNS

102
WHO KNOWS THE NOSE?

1. CAT
2. HORSE
3. COW
4. KOALA
5. HAMSTER
6. PIG
7. RABBIT
8. HIPPO
9. DEER
10. WALRUS
11. HEDGEHOG
12. MONKEY
13. SEA LION
14. SLOTH
15. CAMEL
16. GOAT

103
AWESOME BLOSSOMS

Answers

105
DINNER SCRAMBLE

SOUP
TACO
STEW
STEAK
CHILI
SALAD
BURGER
STIR FRY
MEATLOAF
SPAGHETTI
FISH STICKS
SLOPPY JOES

What did the dog serve with dinner?
A BOTTLE OF FETCH-UP.

106
PAIR OF PIES

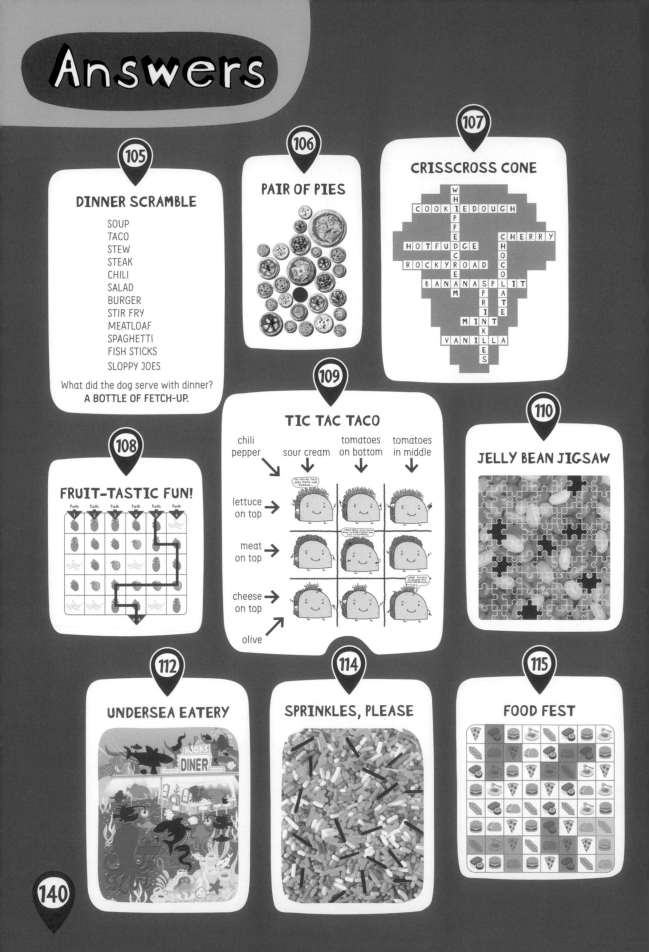

107
CRISSCROSS CONE

108
FRUIT-TASTIC FUN!

109
TIC TAC TACO

110
JELLY BEAN JIGSAW

112
UNDERSEA EATERY

114
SPRINKLES, PLEASE

115
FOOD FEST

Answers

117
MEET YOUR TOUR GUIDE!

118
ASTRO ADVENTURE

There are more blue stars.

Riddle 1
NOT IN A MILLION YEARS.

Riddle 2
YOU ROCKET.

Riddle 3
BECAUSE IT WAS FULL.

Riddle 4
UNIDENTIFIED FRYING OBJECTS.

Unscramble this word to find out what kind of puzzle solver you are:
STELLAR!

119
HOME SWEET HOME
Zig: Hot planet; red ship
Vot: Cold planet; blue ship
Spo: Wet planet; yellow ship

124
COSMIC CODE
HELLO, HELLO, HELLO!

BUT I HAVEN'T HAD BREAKFAST YET.

ROASTING MARTIAN-MALLOWS.

IT'S OUT OF THIS WORLD!

120
ROCKET SHIP WORD SEARCH

121
SPACE QUIZ
1. A
2. C
3. B
4. C
5. A
6. B

125
TIC TAC PLANET

clouds   stripes   rocket ship   moons

red spots →

stars →

blue and green →

ring →

128
SPACE PUZZLER
1. ECLIPSE
2. JUPITER
3. PLANET
4. GALAXY
5. SATURN
6. BLACK HOLE
7. SOLAR FLARE
8. SOLAR SYSTEM
9. COMET
10. BIG DIPPER

How does the solar system tell jokes?
WITH A LOT OF STARCASM.

126
COMICS MIX-UP
1. A
2. B
3. D
4. C

Answers

129
STARGAZING

130
TUNE-UP SPOT

133
HERE COMES THE SUN

If the sun were the size of a door in your house, how big would Earth be?
THE SIZE OF A NICKEL.

134
FAR FROM HOME

How do you have a good outer-space party?
PLAN-ET.

ILLUSTRATIONS AND PHOTOS

Illustration Credits Travis Foster (8, 22–23, 76, 108); Kevin Zimmer (9, 34, 67, 68); Victor Medina (20); Kelly Kennedy (21, 44, 74–75); Jennifer Harney (24); Jim Bradshaw (27–29, 109, 124); Rich Powell (31); Mitch Mortimer (32, 108, 112, 122–123); Jim Paillot (33); Robert L. Prince (34); Avram Dumitrescu (35); Jared Andrew Schorr (36); Brian Michael Weaver (26, 39, 90–91); Luke Flowers (42); Tim Davis (43); Sebastian Abboud (57); Christopher Hart (58); Ron Zalme (59); Tim Beaumont (67); Mike Dammer (68); Steve Skelton (72–73); Joel Santana (79); Gary LaCoste (82–83); Shaw Nielsen (85); Jackie Stafford (94); Tom Woolley (97); Carolina Farias (98); Andy Romanchik (100); Erin Hunting (101); Pintachan (103); Dave Whamond (113); Tim Wesson (117); David Coulson (118); Jim Steck (119); Garry Colby (120); Paul Richer (125); Chuck Dillon (127, 129); David Helton (130); R. Sikoryak (134) *Stock Image Credits* iStock/Getty Images Plus (inside front/back covers, 2–3, 37, 38, 43, 46, 62, 65, 66, 71, 84, 86–87, 102, 106, 111, 114, 132–133); iStock/Getty Images (9, 81); DigitalVision Vectors/halepak (37); MuchMania (37); Jupiterimages Corporation (40–41) iStock Editorial/Getty Images Plus (43, 60); Getty Images (89, 96, 115); Thinkstock (99); Jupiterimages/Thinkstock (99); Comstock/Thinkstock (99)

Cover art by Sr. Sanchez

For information about permission to reprint selections from this book, please contact permissions@highlights.com.

Published by Highlights Press
815 Church Street
Honesdale, Pennsylvania 18431
ISBN: 978-1-64472-923-6
Manufactured in Dongguan, Guangdong, China
Mfg. 12/2023

First edition
Visit our website at Highlights.com.
10 9 8 7 6 5 4 3 2 1

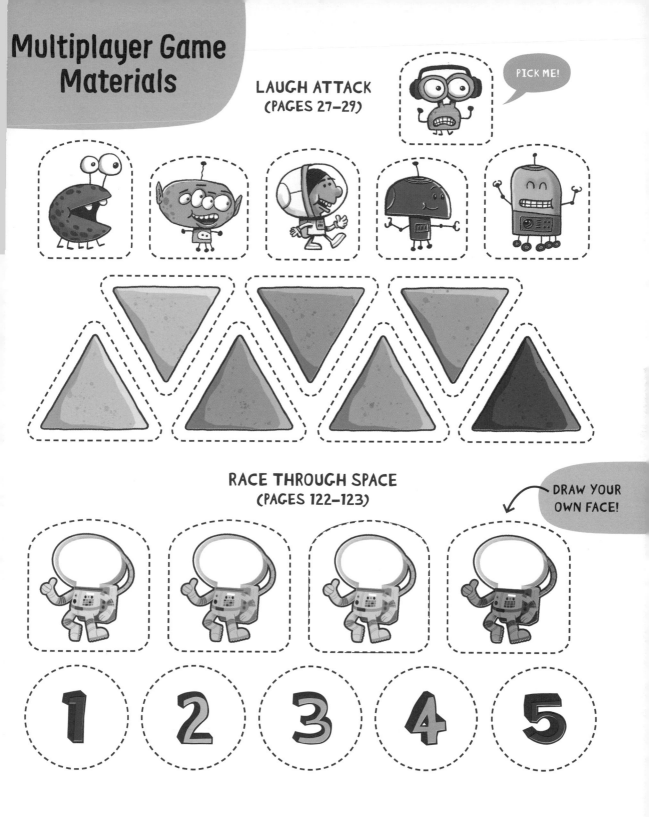